CLASS

CLASS

WHERE DO YOU STAND?

GREG HADFIELD

&

MARK SKIPWORTH

BLOOMSBURY

First published in 1994 by
Bloomsbury Publishing Ltd
2 Soho Square
London, W1V 5DE

Copyright © by Greg Hadfield and Mark Skipworth 1994
The moral right of the authors has been asserted
A copy of the CIP entry for this book is available from the
British Library

ISBN 0 7475 1688 X
10 9 8 7 6 5 4 3 2 1

Text designed by Geoff Green
Typeset by Hewer Text Composition Services, Edinburgh
Printed in Britain by Clays Ltd, St Ives plc

CONTENTS

'The history of all hitherto existing society is
the history of class struggles'
– Karl Marx and Friedrich Engels,
The Communist Party Manifesto (1848)

'A genuinely classless society in which people
can rise to whatever level that their own
abilities and good fortune may take them, from
whatever their starting point'
– John Major's vision, (1990)

CHAPTER ONE

—

KEEPING UP WITH THE JONESES

*T*AKE a name like Jones: typically British, outstandingly anonymous, a byword for the ordinary. In a nation where an average of 600 people crowd into every square mile, you can count on finding at least half a dozen Joneses every few hundred yards. They are just as likely to populate the factory shop-floor in Barnsley as the boardroom in the City; they inhabit suburban semis in Solihull, council flats in Coventry, and country houses in the Cotswolds; their children rub shoulders with the wealthy at Eton and Oxbridge, compete for academic honours at the local grammar school or plate-glass university for the upwardly mobile, and slouch in the back row of classrooms in run-down inner-city comprehensives. So contrasting are their lifestyles, their backgrounds, their tastes, their accents, their income and their spending habits that it is as if they live worlds apart, on opposite sides of the same universe.

Bring them together and, in a room full of strangers, what is the first question they ask each other? As likely as not, it will be, 'So what do you do for a living?'; possibly, it will be, 'Where do you live?' or 'Where do you come from?' or 'Which school did you go to?' In America they would be more direct: 'How much do you earn?' is the question that commonly helps to break the ice at Manhattan dinner parties. Indeed, the phrase 'Keeping up with the Joneses' was coined as the title of a 1913 comic strip in the New York *Globe*; it was another 20 years before it became common usage in Britain.

Call it routine small talk, established etiquette, or simply idle curiosity. As familiarity grows, the list of questions lengthens, even if some are dressed in an innocent getting-to-know-you guise: Where are you going on holiday? Have you seen any good films lately? What sort of car do you drive? Which newspaper do you read? By the way, is that an Armani suit? In the vortex of an increasingly complex society, we all struggle to establish an affinity with 'people like us' – or like we imagine ourselves to be; more importantly, we search for an affinity with those who are like the people we want to be. We are also quick to lump the rest into 'people like that' or 'you know, that sort of person'.

Questions of class remain a peculiarly British obsession. It used to be a lot simpler – and not that long ago. You grew up surrounded by people who lived in the same sort of houses; you worked in the same local offices, shops or factories with people who earned roughly similar wages; and you spent a fixed amount of money on the necessities of life and a strictly limited range of luxuries. For the mass of the population there were few options. People rarely moved house or job, except within a narrowly defined geographical area; there were no credit cards, no designer-label fashions, no package holidays, and only a couple of television channels; owning a car was a distinction in itself, and it did not matter too much what kind of car it was. Do you remember the first person in your street to get a colour television set? Can you recall the schoolfriends whose parents had a telephone – and those who didn't? In those days, advertisers peddled products more than dreams; they concentrated on appealing to the material needs of potential customers rather than nurturing the ambitions of aspiring consumers.

In the end, class is really about choice. The higher up the social ladder you are, the more choices you can afford and the more you are offered; how you exercise those choices determines how much higher up the social ladder you climb. As the number of options increases, the trick is to know which are the right ones to choose. For almost everybody since the industrial revolution, what you did for a living determined where you stood in society and what you could achieve in it. Your job – even regardless of how much you earned – dictated how others regarded you and how you regarded yourself.

There was no talk about 'lifestyle', simply because people in the same street or the same part of town shared the same sort of lives. The boundaries between classes were clear, and few crossed them. Broadly, there was a place for everybody and everybody knew his or her place. In 1949, when Gallup pollsters gave people the chance to describe their class position, 43% said they were working-class and 52% said they were, to some degree, middle-class. The middle-class respondents were a discerning crowd: 16% said they were 'lower middle class'; 29% described themselves as 'middle middle class'; 7% were 'upper middle class'.

How did they know, and were they right? What are the rules of the game, and who made them up? The ability to recognise the similarities and differences between individuals is a defining human characteristic; its origins go back to when our ape-like ancestors became conscious they were individuals and not simply part of a tribe or herd. Ever since, rulers have consistently divided people for their own ends, whether to exploit them, woo them or help them.

From the philosopher-kings of Plato to the enlightened oligarchies of Aristotle, some of the world's greatest thinkers have strived to categorise society. In ancient times Servius Tullius, the semi-legendary sixth king of Rome, divided the Roman people into five 'classes', according to wealth, for taxation purposes. Philosophers have grouped people to explain the past and illuminate the present, or even predict the future. Thomas Hobbes, writing during the English Civil War, believed that all men were equal and that there was no cohesive class system, only individuals who had to be regulated by a powerful state. John Locke, on the other hand, spurred by the challenge to aristocratic rule from an upstart bourgeoisie, maintained there was a fundamental division between different classes, between property-owners and labourers.

In the 19th century Karl Marx went further. Diagnosis became prognosis as Marx envisaged a future society increasingly divided into 'two great classes directly facing each other: bourgeoisie and proletariat'; the subsequent dictatorship of the proletariat, according to Marx, would mark the transition to the abolition of all classes and to a classless society. He was wrong about that, but he was right about the power that class exerts and the changing nature of classes. The seeds, however, of an iconoclastic struggle between collectivism and individualism were already being sown in the works of Friedrich Wilhelm Nietzsche and his 'cult of the individual'. Superman took on Everyman.

Through the ages philosophers, economists and pundits – usually, to a man, from the 'professional middle classes' – have attempted to fool us into thinking that they can measure our class with scientific accuracy, as if taking our temperature or measuring how tall we are. In their eyes, we are all bit-part players in a broader tableau. It is all down either to what job we do, or how much we earn, or what sort of school we went to, or how we talk, or even

3

whether we have a double-barrelled surname. Old-fashioned definitions of class, however, are not only a method of attempting to
describe society; they are also about reassuring the privileged few of
their supposed superiority, while preventing others from getting
ideas above their station. In some cases, particularly those on the
boundaries between classes, the old-fashioned approach does both
at the same time. How grateful are the 'lower middle classes' that
they are no longer working class! Even shop-floor workers take
solace in the nice pretensions of the social hierarchy: 'The working
class can kiss my ass, I've got the foreman's job at last.' For such
people, Dr Johnson got it about right. 'We are,' he pronounced, 'by
our occupations, education, and habits of life, divided almost into
different species, which regard one another, for the most part, with
scorn and malignity.' He could have added envy, jealousy, admira-
tion, or almost any other human emotion.

The picture that all existing class definitions has created is so
static that it is the sociological equivalent of a still-life painting. It is
also like a jigsaw, a very simple pyramid-shaped one of the sort a six-
year-old could do. It comprises a handful of slab-like pieces, each
one a different size, but all apparently fitting so neatly together that it
is as if God intended it that way. In each slab millions of us are
imprisoned – or cocooned, if you are at, or near, the summit. This
has led some rebellious souls to condemn class as 'a bad thing' and
wish it away like demons in the night. It is a pointless exercise: class
divisions are here to stay, but they are no longer the prisons that
were fashioned in a bygone era by an Establishment that has now
had its day. They are rungs on a ladder that extends from the
bottom to the top of a society in which the gap between rich and
poor is widening; we journey up and down it week by week, and year
by year.

It is time to play by different rules. The social classifications in use
today were first officially defined more than 80 years ago in the
Upstairs, Downstairs world of Edwardian snobbery. They emerged
out of a furious and fashionable debate about eugenics, the study of
improving the quality of the human race by selective breeding. In
1913 Dr T.H.C. Stevenson, a medical statistician, came up with a
five-grade classification based on occupations; initially, there were
separate categories for agriculture, coal-mining and textiles.

At its heart, however, were three clearly defined classes: Class I –
'the upper and middle class'; Class III – 'those occupations of which

it can be assumed that the majority of men (*sic*) classified to them ... are skilled workmen'; and Class V – 'occupations including mainly unskilled workmen'. In between were sandwiched two vaguely defined classes that were neither one nor the other.

It was hardly scientific and inevitably reflected a lot of prejudice on the part of those responsible for deciding, for example, that an academic was higher up the pecking order than a businessman. It assumed that manual workers were a different and inferior breed, while pen-pushing clerical workers, along with professionals and other non-manual workers, were put in the top drawer of society; within 20 years, the pen-pushers had been relegated to the third division. Although little is known about the classification's lengthy and somewhat haphazard development over more than two decades, it is clear it was concocted for the specific purpose of analysing whether a decline in the birth rate was having a bigger impact on the professional middle classes than on the working classes, and was first employed to compare rates of infant mortality in different sections of society. Both were hot issues in the aftermath of the government's Inquiry on Physical Deterioration, launched in response to the reverses of the Boer War!

From such an arcane background springs the everyday language of class; the As, the Bs, the C1s, the C2s, the Ds and the Es. The As are the professionals, the senior civil servants and the captains of industry or commerce; the Bs are the managers and the bureaucrats; the C1s are the office workers, the owners of small businesses and all the others who do not earn a living by getting their hands dirty. Lower down the scale are the C2s, Ds and Es, what we like to call the manual working class.

Needless to say, the world has changed since the British Empire was humbled by rebellious Afrikaaners. 'Let us be frank about it: most of our people have never had it so good,' Harold Macmillan, the then prime minister said in 1957. The watershed was the Second World War, won by working-class soldiers led by middle-class officers. Then, both classes were determined to win the peace, and a share of the affluence that followed. Nancy Mitford's intrinsically reactionary *Noblesse Oblige*, published the year before Macmillan's remarks, provided the ultimate snob's guide to post-war aristocracy and attempted, teasingly, to stem a tide that was turning against unquestioning deference to social superiors. In the decade of Suez and Aden and the sunset of the British Empire, the old order was starting to lose its grip. In 1955 the British 'Establishment' was given its name in a phrase popularised by Henry Fairlie in an article in the *Spectator*. Give the enemy a name and let battle begin. Two years earlier the historian A.J.P. Taylor had written: 'The Establishment talks with its own branded accents; eats different meals at different times; has its privileged system of education; its own religion, even – to a large extent – its own form of football . . . There is nothing more agreeable in life than to make peace with the Establishment – and nothing more corrupting.'

Now, in the twilight of the second Elizabethan age, the defining institution of the nation – and the one that endorsed and legitimised the Establishment and the old class system – is in crisis. The monarchy is suffering because the disguise of our disguised republic, and the Commonwealth of which it is the head, is wearing thin. It has been fundamentally weakened by a crisis of confidence among its subjects and a crisis of self-confidence among its own. The Royal Family, increasingly middle class in its membership, tastes and attitudes, is no longer revered as distant, aloof or even that special: the royals visit Disneyland, go skiing at Klosters, play golf, admire Lloyd Webber musicals, swoon to pop songs by George Michael or Phil Collins, eat organic food, dine with the likes of Billy Connolly and Pamela Stephenson, sunbathe on Caribbean islands, have plebeian views on architecture and may even secretly enjoy the Royal Command variety shows. Its members have affairs and get divorced; they embrace outsiders from the middle class but cannot absorb or tame them; the Queen pays taxes and her children play at getting jobs; like the proverbial emperor, the princes and princesses are shown, quite literally at times, to have no clothes. Newspapers, both tabloid and broadsheet, revel in the mobile-phone-calling, toe-sucking, tear-jerking, gym-exercising, theme-park-visiting, bulimia-suffering celebrities who star in the Buckingham Palace soap opera.

The cumulative effect of Squidgygate, Fergiegate and Camillagate has been to replace deference with popular disdain, even among the working class whose loyalty, historically, has been fundamental to the strength of constitutional monarchy. 'Above all things our royalty is to be reverenced,' Walter Bagehot, the economist and essayist, wrote in the mid-19th century, 'and if you begin to poke about it, you cannot reverence it . . . Its mystery is its life. We must not let in daylight upon magic.' The old magic has gone: the working-class audience that the royal family relied upon for support has largely evaporated, and its pursuit of a new middle-class identity to win the allegiance of the new middle class is doomed to failure.

Within a generation, the economy has been transformed, standards of living have soared, manufacturing industry has declined, service industries have mushroomed, technology has made itself felt in every part of modern life, both at work and in the home; even the lie of the land has taken on a different appearance from urban and suburban sprawl, rural poverty, inner-city degeneration and the 'yuppification' of once-deprived areas. Even though it is the old middle class that has often benefited disproportionately from these changes, members of the old working class are also much better off, both materially and culturally. As a result, they have been able to follow careers they might never have dreamed of, acquire possessions that either had not been invented 20 years ago or were the exclusive property of the higher-ups, and they have enough disposable income, credit-card flexibility and leisure to take part in pastimes and activities from which they were previously excluded. The implications are clear: the fabric of society is now woven on a different loom.

Typically, salaries have doubled within a generation. Ten million people own shares, compared with fewer than 3 million when Margaret Thatcher, mother of the upwardly mobile, came to power. The amount of disposable income per head of population is at record levels, nearly four-fifths higher than in 1971. Consumer spending has more than doubled in cash terms in a decade, with the sharpest increases on school fees, medical insurance, leisure activities and domestic help. The amount of credit has trebled since 1976; twice as many houses are owner-occupied than in 1961.

More than 1 million council tenants have bought their homes; the proportion of people owning their homes has risen from 29% to 67% in 40 years. As a result, the amount of heritable wealth – currently £14 billion a year – is expected to rise to £35 billion a year within the current generation. In 1992, an average of nearly 5p in every £1 of income was saved, the highest level since records began; more than 7 million people are covered by private medical insurance, nearly a sevenfold increase since 1966; the package-holiday generation has raised its sights towards ever more exotic destinations, with a quarter of families taking two or more holidays each year – three times the proportion 25 years ago; the number of foreign holidays has quadrupled to a record 22 million a year; mobile phones, only recently a fashion accessory for status-conscious yuppies, have become a tool of the trade for plumbers, gas-fitters and electricians everywhere; the number of students in higher education is 1.3 million, twice what it was in 1971; Oxbridge now takes nearly as many state school pupils as public school pupils; since 1978 trade union membership has fallen from 13.3 million to 9.9 million, from 53% of the labour force to 38%. At the same time, the old order and the certainty that it encouraged has all but disappeared. 'White-collar' workers have learned what it is like to fear recession and redundancy; 'blue-collar' counterparts are increasingly the beneficiaries of executive-style perks. All this and still our class position, we are told by the experts, is determined simply by what we do for a living.

So what did MORI, the opinion poll company, find after a decade of Thatcherism had sown the seeds for the biggest social change this century? Pollsters asked the same question about class that Gallup had asked 40 years earlier. They found more than two in three (67%) said they were working class, compared with 43% in 1949; only three in 10 (30%) said they were middle class, compared with Gallup's 52%. We are all middle class now – or at least aspire to be – but more of us than ever seem convinced we are working class! 'The hierarchy of class has changed in reality, but perceptions of the meaning of the hierarchy have changed even more,' concluded Bob Worcester, chairman of MORI. 'In class matters, you are in the end what you think you are.' It would seem, then, that anarchy rules. There is a gulf between how the experts perceive reality and how the rest of us experience it. The reason is that the model of the class structure that has served us so inadequately for the best part of a century has finally collapsed under the strain of accommodating far-reaching, and probably irreversible, social change. In truth, our 'social identity' is no longer crucially defined by our occupations. In a materialistic society, we are classed according to the quantity and quality of our possessions; in a media culture, we are judged by the newspapers we read, the television we watch, the films we see and the celebrities we lionise. In an all-consuming consumer society, our class position is determined not simply, as Marx held, by our relation to the means of production, but also by our relation to the modes of consumption.

Even though the traditional occupational groupings were not

intended as a rigorous index of social class, and even though they were created to meet the needs of a bygone era, they have survived not as a relic but as a national monument, a part of our intellectual heritage that must not be challenged. There are scores of variations - many of them inspired by the rise of the market-research industry since the 1950s – but almost all are directly derived from the original five-grade hierarchy. It has two obvious advantages: it is simple – when market researchers or opinion pollsters stop you in the street, it takes them roughly one minute and four questions to pigeonhole you – and it has been around long enough to allow comparisons over the past eight decades, even though they are largely meaningless because the fine detail of the classifications has been constantly revised, refined and generally tinkered with. As new jobs emerge and old ones disappear, there is tremendous latitude for redefining the occupational boundaries: unlike Britain, the arbiters in the United States appear to be more willing to put the new occupations – those in computing and technology, for example – in the higher social classes, reinforcing the view of an affluent American 'can-do' society in which the class pyramid is gradually being turned on its head, with more and more people congregating towards the top.

The new British system of Standard Occupational Classification, introduced for the 1991 census and requiring its own computer software package for it to be used easily, comprises 18 'major' occupational groups and 73 'minor' ones, within which it distinguishes 378 'occupational unit groups' and 3,800 occupations. Not surprisingly, the Market Research Society, with more than 7,000 members who work in the £350 million-a-year industry, has promoted the alternative, simplified classification system used by the Institute of Practitioners in Advertising. It is based on the occupation of the head of the household, usually male, and enshrined in a 'jobs dictionary' allocating a social class to everybody from admirals (As) and acrobats (C1s) to moderately qualified zoologists (Bs) and semi-skilled zinc-workers (Ds). There are even mentions for almoners (Bs), barrowboys (Ds) and hedge-builders (C2s). Just about the most significant difference compared with 80 years ago is that both of today's most widely used 'class ladders' have six rungs instead of the original five. In essence, though, they still reflect the prejudices and preconceptions common among late-Victorian or Edwardian professional gentlemen surveying British society at the start of the 20th century.

HOW THE GOVERNMENT PUTS YOU IN YOUR PLACE

Class		% of adults
I	Professional occupations	5
II	Managerial and technical occupations	28
III(N)	Skilled occupations: non-manual	23
III(M)	Skilled occupations: manual	21
IV	Partly skilled occupations	15
V	Unskilled occupations	6

Source: *1991 Census*, OPCS. Members of the armed forces and those whose occupation was inadequately described or unstated account for 2% of the population.

HOW MARKET RESEARCHERS COMPARE ON CLASS

Class	% of heads of households
A Upper middle class (e.g. Professional, higher managerial, senior civil servants)	3
B Middle class (e.g. middle managers, principal officers in local/central government)	16
C1 Lower middle class (e.g. junior managers, routine white-collar or non-manual workers)	26
C2 Skilled working class (e.g. skilled manual workers)	26
D Semi-skilled and unskilled working class (e.g. manual workers, apprentices to skilled workers)	17
E Residual (e.g. those dependent on long-term state benefits)	13

Source: *National Readership Survey*, NRS Ltd, July 1992–July 1993

So what are the main faults with current definitions of class that, on the face of it at least, provide a credible snapshot of society at large? First of all, they are remarkably crude. Indeed, as we shall see, they are virtually useless when it comes down to individuals. They are designed to help statisticians discover general truths and to enable market researchers and advertisers to target mass audiences; even then, with a big enough sample, they can differentiate only between six broad categories in a population of 58 million. The heavy-handedness of the current classification is in stark contrast to the sensitivity needed to make sense of where you fit into a complex hierarchy compared with, say, your next-door neighbours, friends, colleagues or relatives. It is a jigsaw in which we are all pieces, but we are not told precisely where any of the pieces go, and none of them fits exactly anyway. It is all very well learning that we are somewhere in the premier league, or the first division or whatever. But where exactly? And are we pushing for promotion or struggling to stave off relegation?

Secondly, current definitions are entirely one-dimensional. Our class, we are told officially, is determined exclusively by what we are doing now, not what we have done in the past or aspire to do in the future. It takes no account of our background – where we have come from – nor our ambitions, which inevitably shape what is to come. Even in the present, no account is taken of the qualifications we have, our cultural tastes, what we do in our spare time, what we read, what we own, or what spare cash we have after we have paid the household bills. It is commonly accepted among market researchers that someone in occupational class C2 or D may have more disposable income than someone in class A, B or C1. 'The financial chains of private education are likely to constrain an AB,' one expert has admitted, 'as much as the black economy and overtime can enhance the apparently lower wage of the C2D.'

Thirdly, many women are classified according to the occupations of their partner as 'heads of household': a high-flying career-woman, possibly an A or B, could find herself pigeonholed as a C2 if she happens to be married to a semi-skilled bricklayer. With the rise to prominence of women in all areas of public life, and the weakening of the traditional family unit and the ties that bind it together, the concept of men ruling the roost as 'heads of household' is ludicrously obsolete; family members increasingly lead their own lives, to such an extent that even the family meal is becoming a thing of the past. About half of working women would be classified differently by their own occupation, and by early in the 21st century it is expected that the typical worker will be a woman who works part time and therefore would fit unsatisfactorily into the traditional classifications. It is only recently that some researchers have begun, just as arbitrarily, to classify people, just as simplistically, according to the occupation of the 'chief wage-earner': more than 600,000 people are chief wage-earners in households of which they are not the head. No specific account, though, is taken of earnings: a miner (C2) paid more than £30,000 a year is automatically regarded as the inferior of a schoolteacher who may be earning less than half that amount. A vicar on a pittance can be the same class as a lawyer on a six-figure salary; when the student daughter of the lawyer leaves home to share a flat with friends, she is a C1; if the student daughter of the vicar stays at home in the vicarage during her studies, she is classed as a B. The Duke of Westminster, who happens to be the richest man in Britain, has to accept he will be classed among the professional and managerial middle classes; there is no separate category for the aristocracy, on the grounds it is too small to be of statistical significance.

There is the additional problem of what sociologists call 'contradictory class locations'. They like to think these are the exceptions that prove the rule: the chairman of a blue-chip company who did not go to Oxbridge but left a state secondary modern at 16; the London taxi driver who loves opera, has a PhD in history, and goes hunting at weekends; or the City stockbroker who reads the *Sun*, stands on the terraces at Stamford Bridge and likes nothing better than a pint of bitter while propping up the bar at the Dog and Duck. Now, however, the 'exceptions' are increasingly the rule. There is a new élite from a different mould and with a different social inheritance. They are the front-line class warriors who make the most of the meritocratic chinks in the Establishment's tarnished armour. Even at a more modest level, there are people every day breaking free from the class-ridden straitjacket: the working-class ex-grammar school pupils who make it to the top of their professions; the 11-plus 'failures' from council estates who become prosperous entrepreneurs; the City whizzkids who never went to public school or Oxbridge. The social ladder is getting longer, extending further down into society and stretching all the way to the top. It is also getting much slipperier and, with the bankruptcy and pretensions of the old élite more readily exposed, more people are joining the ranks of the downwardly mobile. Consequently, a more sophisticated instrument is needed to measure the social class both of those climbing the ladder and those sliding – or tumbling – down it.

Even by its own criteria, how accurate or consistent is the traditional method of measuring class, anyway? There is ample evidence that the most experienced arbiters of class can easily get it wrong, and regularly do. When researchers studying the composition of television audiences found that up to one in three viewers apparently changed their occupational class in 12 months, they quickly decided to go back to the drawing board. Their revised figure was put at somewhere between one in 25 and one in 14.

Another survey found 'startling' evidence of just how often people are put in the wrong class. Sarah O'Brien, research manager at Granada Television, said the findings placed 'substantial question marks over current industry practice concerning social class'. The 1988 survey, involving 50-minute face-to-face interviews, questioned 1,380 adults to discover full details about occupations, disposable income, financial holdings, possessions and leisure activities. Expert interviewers questioned about a third of the initial sample again 10 months later. On the surface, little appeared to have changed: the proportion of As, Bs, C1s and so on remained the same. On closer study, however, it emerged that 41% of those questioned had actually been re-allocated to a different class – and nearly one in three (30%) of these had moved up or down by two notches.

About one quarter of the changes were genuine and rational, including a milkman (D) who had started work for an agricultural mineral service company (C1). Others were bizarre: a 55-year-old woman, living alone and unemployed and therefore an E to begin with, rose up the social scale simply because her son, an assembler in a car manufacturing company (C2), returned to live at home and became chief wage-earner; a managing director (A) of a clothing company employing 80 people had left to set up his own company but had not yet begun to take on any staff, and was thus a C1. In a comment remarkable for its understatement, O'Brien concluded: 'Social class is not, of course, intended to reflect income precisely, but one cannot help feeling that the technically correct upward shift of a household because the head of household (a winder in a mine, C2) is no longer working and his daughter (a nurse, C1) becomes chief wage-earner, gives a rather misleading picture of the household's economic position.' Even among those where the head of household's job had remained the same, researchers still found nearly four in 10 had apparently changed class. The biggest problems were with the Ds and Es, O'Brien said: 'If a 41% apparent change can be recorded using this detailed approach, one wonders what might be occurring where the guidance given to interviewers is less detailed.'

It is no surprise, then, to learn that advertisers, credit-card companies, market researchers and glitzy journalists on glossy magazines have sought alternative ways of categorising people. Most of them are either just as one-dimensional as occupational class or so vaguely defined that they evaporate as soon as you try to examine their substance. Age or 'lifestage' are particularly fashionable as defining characteristics; others employ residential neighbourhoods – 'Wealthy Achievers, Suburban Areas', 'Affluent Greys, Rural Communities', and so on – to locate clusters of people with similar attributes; some use lifestyle groupings such as 'Sociable Spenders', 'Prudent Affluent', or 'Acquisitors'. Many such groupings, however, appear to be little more than acronyms in search of a meaning:

Yuppies: Young, upwardly mobile professionals. A phenomenon of the 1980s and showing signs of a resurgence in the 1990s, their trade marks were richly coloured Porsches, mobile phones and a 'greed-is-good' creed that put a premium on career success.

Yaks: Young, adventurous, keen and single. Aged 18 to 24, they are said to live at home or rent flats; with no heavy financial burdens, they are status-seekers distinguished by a taste for designer-label clothes, Mediterranean suntans and winter skiing in fashionable Swiss or American resorts. They love eating out, but keep themselves in trim with regular visits to the health club.

Ewes: Experts with expensive style. By the age of 25 to 34, they are high-flying trendsetters, often couples with two incomes, a first mortgage and no children. They are said to spend heavily on the home and enjoy hectic social lives with other Ewes.

Bats: Babies add the sparkle. Similar to Ewes, they are married or living together, with a mortgage and children. Most of their cash goes on their house and family. They have to balance their books and use credit cards responsibly. For holidays, they go camping in France, or stay at a friend's cottage in the country, particularly Devon or Norfolk.

Clams: Carefully look at most spending. Aged 34 to 44, the so-called Clams have older children. They may be divorcing, remarrying, or going through a mid-life crisis; they may be doing all three. Although they have high incomes, they have huge bills to match, including big mortgages and expensive school fees. As high borrowers, they have to watch which way the cash flows.

Their social life is dominated by dinner parties with friends who also cannot afford to eat out; second-hand estate cars are a favourite means of transport.

Mice: Money is coming easier. In their 40s or early 50s, their children have started to leave home and their mortgage is almost paid off. High disposable incomes, which help pay for regular holidays, are frequently supplemented by family inheritances.

Owls: Older with less stress. The over-55s who have paid off their mortgages or moved to more modest homes. Their biggest spending goes on gifts and, yes, holidays – whether it is a coach trip in the Highlands of Scotland or trans-global trekking.

Some of these groupings are clearly meant as jokes and are dreamed up merely to fill column inches in tabloid newspapers and the even bigger void in tabloid minds. They include: **Sitcoms** – Single Income, Two Children, Outrageous Mortgage; **Grumps** – Grim, Ruthless, Upwardly Mobile Professionals; **Dinks** – Double Income, No Kids; **Oinks** – One Income, No Kids; **Ticks** – Two-Income Couples with Kids; **Dwiks** – Dual Income with Kids; **Minks** – Multiple Income, No Kids; **Bobos** – Burnt Out But Opulent; **Nopes** – Not Out-wardly Prosperous Educated Persons; **Spom** – Success with Peace of Mind; **Pippy** – Person Inheriting Parents' Property; **Swell** – Single Woman Earning Lots of Lolly; **Opals** – Older People with Active Lifestyles.

Other lifestyle or 'lifestage' approaches are more scientific, although they seldom cover more than 80% of the population. More importantly, each group or class, usually based on spending power, is still too large for the individuals within it to compare themselves with other class members. Crucially, there is no clear rank order of the various groups:

Granny Power: Aged 55 to 70, people in households where neither the head of the household 'nor the housewife' works full time. They have no children or dependants (14% of the adult population).

Grey Power: Aged 45 to 60, households where either the head of the household or 'the housewife' is working full time. No children and no dependants (12% of the adult population).

Older Silver Power: Married people with children aged five to 15 (18% of the adult population).

Young Silver Power: People who are married, with children aged four or younger (16% of the adult population).

Platinum Power: Married people aged 40 or under, with no children (7% of the adult population).

Golden Power: Single people aged 40 or under, with no children (15% of the adult population).

In a world that is recreated daily in the image of a global village, the media you choose to consume is regarded by some as a measure of what sort of person you are and, most importantly for the people who develop such concepts, what particular brand of product or service you are most likely to buy. In 1990 Laing Henry, the London advertising agency, turned its back on existing descriptions and came up with BATS: Brand Advertising Targeting System. Its fundamental thesis was that what counts is what you read, watch on television and listen to on the radio. Traditional classifications are used simply because they are easy to measure, says Derick Walker, a Laing Henry executive who helped create the system: 'However, they don't take account of individual values, and nowadays we tend to want to be different from the Joneses.' The creators of BATS point out that in Britain in the 1980s there were 20 new television channels, 20 new national newspaper sections, 64 new radio stations and 3,000 new magazines. You *are* the media you consume, they argued. A year-long analysis of media habits, attitudes and 'product consumption' of 24,000 adults generated a dozen broad groupings. The four biggest give a taste of what Laing Henry is getting at:

Soaps and Sun: People who live in council houses and watch ITV, especially soap operas, *Blind Date* and anything with Jeremy Beadle in it – mainly housewives, readers of *Woman's Own* and *Chat*, married with young children. They eat beefburgers and ice-cream, and drink instant coffee; they take package holidays to sun-kissed destinations and see Shirley Valentine as a role-model (15% of the population).

Telly Dawn to Dusk: Those aged over 55, not working and likely to be widowed. They watch television all day long from breakfast time to the latest late show. They live in rented homes, have a meagre income of only a few thousand pounds a year, hate exotic food and love shopping and housework. They drive a Ford and are old enough to keep alive the memory of Dandy Nicholls, Alf

Garnett's wife, as a role-model (13% of the population).

Mainstream Media Rejectors: These people don't watch much television and when they do it is usually the news or programmes such as *Tomorrow's World*. They are often southern-based graduates who do not read many newspapers but like to flick through *New Scientist*; they are home-owners with school-age children and an annual income of £30,000 or so; they prefer health food to junk food and care about green issues, drive Fiat Unos, and model themselves on the likes of Richard Briers in the television sit-com *The Good Life* (13% of the population).

Genteel Media Grazers: Live in rural areas and watch a lot of ITV and Channel Four, especially game shows; with an income of less than £6,000 a year, they read the *Sporting Life*, never go to the cinema and, in fact, rarely go out at all; they don't drive, don't use credit cards, are house-proud, like gardening and prefer drinking tea to alcohol; they eat chocolates and fresh fish, presumably separately. If they have a role-model, it will be someone like Mrs Goggins in *Postman Pat* (13% of the population).

So what is class really determined by? Jobs are obviously still important, but so are spending habits, lifestyles, education, housing and leisure activities. Like beauty, class is largely in the eye of the beholder; like beauty also, we can all make the most of what we have and put on the best face possible to the rest of the world. Whether self-consciously or sub-consciously, we can aspire to, or assume, a class position that may be higher than others would automatically ascribe to us.

In the autumn of 1993 ICM Research conducted a survey for the *Scotsman* newspaper. Although all the interviews were conducted in Scotland, there is no reason to think the answers are peculiar to that part of the United Kingdom. Of 1,004 people questioned, three in 10 said they thought of themselves as belonging to a particular class, with men being slightly more class-conscious than women, and occupational C2s being slightly more class-conscious than others. Again, two in three (67%) said they were working class; one in four (24%) described themselves as middle class; one in 11 (9%) did not know; retired people were most likely to describe themselves as working class. Remarkably, though, nearly four in 10 of those in occupational classes A or B – such as judges, professors, stockbrokers and psychiatrists – described themselves as working class;

conversely, one in seven in classes D or E – including unskilled manual workers – were convinced they were middle class. It seems that many people are ashamed of being middle class in the same way as many used to be embarrassed about being working class.

JUST WHO DO WE THINK WE ARE?

Occupational class	Percentages		
Those who say they are:	Middle class	Working class	Don't know
AB	51	39	9
AB/C1	39	52	9
C2	18	72	10
DE	14	78	8
All	**24**	**67**	**9**

Source: *The Scotsman*/ICM Research Ltd, September 1993.

Those taking part were asked to pick two or three criteria, from a list of 10, that they would use to judge a person's social class. Where someone lives was most frequently mentioned, by a total of more than one in three people (36%). Although it was closely followed by someone's occupation, the findings make it obvious that the ingredients of class are many and varied. The recipe, according to most people, appears to change depending on which class you are talking about; different criteria are used to determine membership of different classes. When it came to deciding whether or not someone was upper class, wealth was clearly the most important factor, followed by the neighbourhood they lived in, and level of education; for membership of the middle classes and working classes, the most important factors were job, neighbourhood and income. The amount of weight attached to someone's occupation has, however, declined: a similar survey in 1984 found that nearly half the population (46%) used it to define someone's class, compared with just over one in three (31%) less than a decade later.

The art of class-spotting gets more difficult by the day. Leisure activities, voting behaviour and the way people speak have all become less important in the past decade: even the huntin'-shootin'-fishin' fraternity is less homogeneous than it used to be. The new-style Labour party has discovered Filofaxes, silk ties and a fashion for burying its egalitarian roots, while it is estimated that one-third of socialists come from the middle class and six in 10 of those in occupational class A profess to hold socialist values. The rise of 'Estuary English', the native tongue of Essex Man and all his progeny, is nudging the Queen's English aside in the most surprising of places. Even the jobs of the once dinner-jacketed presenters of Radio Three should, according to Liz Forgan (Benenden and Oxford), the head of BBC Radio, be open to people with 'lovely, rich Brummie accents'.

THE BENCHMARKS OF CLASS

What we consider when deciding people's class	
	%
The neighbourhood they live in	36
The job they do	31
How much money they earn	29
How much education they have	27
How wealthy they are	22
The way they talk	17
The clothes they wear	15
Who their parents are	13
How they spend their leisure time	11
Which political party they vote for	11

Source: *The Scotsman*/ICM Research Ltd, September 1993.

Of course, a lot of the clues to class – vocabulary, accent, even demeanour – may appear trivial, so trivial that professional arbiters are reluctant to take them into account. Their importance, however, should not be under-estimated in the skirmishes at the frontiers between social classes. Listen then to Middle England – or, specifically, Anne Giles, of South Croydon in Surrey. She provoked a controversy, of a suitably genteel nature, in the columns of the *Daily Telegraph* after a television reviewer suggested that anyone asking for a 'lavatory' was 'a prat with a speech disorder'. Disgusted of South Croydon was not one to take this lying down: 'I am not a prat, nor have I ever suffered from a speech disorder. This also applies to all those of my friends and relatives who speak as I do. I might also use the words "loo" or "WC", but "toilet" simply does not exist in my vocabulary, as I feel uncomfortable with it.'

In her tirade against inverted snobbery, there were more harsh words: 'I would never refer to a napkin as a "serviette", nor would I use the word "Nan" to describe someone's grandmother: surely a nanny is a person paid to look after one's children? I say "How do you do?" and not "Pleased to meet you", and I never cease to be amazed that children in state schools are taught that their school lunch is a "school dinner" and that the meal they will have in the evening at home is their "tea". And yes, I do pour my tea in first; I also use a tea strainer, napkin rings, fish knives and forks, and I don't hold my knife "that way".' The formidable correspondent, remarkable as much for her resoluteness in defending middle-class niceties as for the quaintness of the niceties themselves, conceded that top people *do* drink coffee 'but not at 4 pm'. At that time of day they usually have tea: Darjeeling, Earl Grey or Lapsang Souchong. Fish knives and napkins are the secret signs of class, as John Betjeman acidly observed in his poetic spoof 'How to Get On in Life':

> Phone for the fish-knives, Norman,
> As Cook is a little unnerved;
> You kiddies have crumpled the serviettes
> And I must have things daintily served.

Famously, John Major, the son of a south London trapeze artist who left school at 16, had a vision. Praising social mobility as one of the great achievements of the Thatcher years, he initiated his campaign for the Tory party leadership in 1990 by saying that 'in the next few years' he wanted 'a genuinely classless society in which people can rise to whatever level that their own abilities and good fortune may take them, from whatever their starting point'. He spoke with feeling as 'one of the people in government who actually remember what a thrill it was when my salary moved up to £2,000 a year'. Since then, he has frequently returned to the theme to express his loathing of snobbery and prejudice, and to assert his determination 'to break down that artificial distinction between the white-collar worker who gets his A-level and goes off to work in a bank and the blue-collar worker who get his vocational training and goes off to be an electrician or a plumber'.

So welcome to Major's 'classless' Britain: the richest 1% of people aged 18 or over own 18% of the nation's £1,694 billion of marketable wealth, a proportion that has remained virtually unchanged since the 1970s; the richest 10% own half of all marketable wealth;

even when 'non-marketable' rights in occupational and state pension schemes are included, the upper echelon's share falls only to 11% and 36%, respectively; more than one-third of personal wealth (36%) is in property; the share of income for the poorest fifth of the population has dropped from 10% to 6% since 1979, while the wealthiest fifth increased its share from 35% to 43%; two-fifths of income is earned by one-fifth of the population, while the bottom fifth earns one-twentieth of all income; uniquely, the real income of the poorest 20%, after housing costs, has actually fallen in the past 15 years. Everyday experience and plain common sense tell you that class is far from dead.

Unsurprisingly, four years after Major's 'classless' pledge, only one in five people believes he has even begun to keep his promise. Part of the lack of faith is down to confusion about what the Prime Minister had in mind. The concepts of a classless society and social mobility sit uneasily together. Suspend disbelief for a moment and suppose there could be a classless society: how would you then have social mobility? How could you measure it and what would it mean? Conversely, if greater social mobility is the ambition, it must depend on increasing the traffic from one class to another. Of course, Major's vision would have more credibility if it had more substance. It is not helping the cause when the end-of-year Downing Street photograph in 1993 featured 23 ministers, of whom 18 went to Cambridge. More than half the 1,150 senior civil servants listed in the latest *Whitehall Companion* directory went to Oxbridge; only five of the 18 permanent secretaries graduated from other universities. In the first honours list of Major's administration, he created the first baronetcy for 30 years with the elevation of Sir Denis Thatcher; in his first 'classless' honours list in 1993, six in 10 recipients came from the top two occupational groups – the highest proportion since he became Tory party leader.

We should not be pessimistic, however. It would be too much to expect the political establishment to be anything but insensitive to social change. Four crucial points must be borne in mind: Britain is still, by any objective measure, a class-ridden and class-conscious society, but opportunities for social mobility by 'class migrants' have never been greater; the simplicity of the 'them-and-us' divisions of the past has been replaced by a more complex, multi-layered class structure; the one-dimensional measurement of class by occupation is obsolete and has to be replaced by a broader three-dimensional approach that takes account of our past, present and future, and embraces all aspects of life outside work; our position within the new class framework is, to a large degree, a matter of subjective judgement and we can, self-consciously and constantly, influence the outcome.

The way class is conventionally defined is only a snapshot, a fleeting moment snatched out of context and categorised in a ready-made hierarchy. The definitions are not elaborate enough or sensitive enough to measure whether you are edging upwards or sinking downwards; they are calibrated only in sudden leaps or slumps. They do not answer the crucial question: are you keeping up with the Joneses? Moreover, class has for too long been regarded as a condition we all suffer from. It is, in fact, a journey that we all travel on; at different times in our lives our position changes, even if our job remains the same. Class is a process that you can participate in; you can, if you wish, transform your position to suit your own ends by changing your lifestyle, tastes and cultural habits. More than ever before, it is possible to escape your background, even though your background never fully leaves you; you can mould your present, if you know what you want and how to get it; and you can choose the sort of person you want to be in future through your ambitions, aspirations and choice of role-models.

Call it social climbing, if you like. Such an artifice, however, has never been sufficient to transcend class barriers; at best, it has been a device to rise to the top of the class in which you find yourself. And if it briefly appears to accomplish more than that, you can be sure that its exponents usually get caught out in the end. As the French historian Alexis de Tocqueville observed, what 'the few' do today 'the many' will do tomorrow: the attitudes and lifestyles of the better-off are good indicators of what will become the norm for the rest when they become similarly well-off later.

Many people change their social class throughout their lives anyway, whether through choice, chance or creeping compromise: the working-class kids who are the first in their family to go to university; the middle-class rebels who become social workers; the career-minded young turks who make a million in the City; the middle-aged executives made redundant in their 50s. Class ambition is not a question of morality or hypocrisy or betrayal; your class roots are important, but roots can be an anchor and a hindrance as well as a source of strength. Since the egalitarian 1960s and 1970s there has been no shame in being working class; now it is the turn of the class-conscious 'middle class' to rid themselves of a sense of guilt.

It is necessary to abandon the old vocabulary of class, to purge it of the out-of-date language that is still employed, whether deliberately or carelessly, to buttress obsolescent class barriers: the useless shorthand that discriminates between 'white-collar' and 'blue-collar' workers; the subtle distinction between salaries and wages; the often inaccurate description of class superiors as 'posh' (believed to derive from 'port out, starboard home', the most desirable locations for voyagers sailing to and from India in the days of the British Raj). Who is posh these days? Is Alan Sugar, the multi-millionaire chairman of Amstrad, posh? Is Anita Roddick, the founder of the Body Shop empire, posh? Even the word 'snob', originally meaning a lower-class person with no pretensions to rank, is a pejorative that lacks clarity.

Class, in its most narrow economic sense, has always been the bedrock of social status; the one arose directly out of the other. Now, however, the two are so intertwined that the distinction is largely meaningless. Your class position is necessarily determined by the subjective measures previously used to establish status; the honour or prestige attached to your occupation; your family background; your cultural position; and your lifestyle. The class struggle is the stuff of history; the position of individuals within it is biography. Class used to provide a sense of belonging, but now it also promises a sense of achievement and distinction. While in the past it was a series of ring-fences that kept people in their place, now it is an all-embracing measure of whether you are succeeding in life.

What is required, therefore, is a holistic approach to class, one that distils all the ingredients that make every individual unique: the sum of all its parts. Such an approach will still throw up 'ideal types' but not the narrow stereotypes generated by the traditional occupational groupings. Among business executives, for example, it will distinguish between the 'ideal types' with six-figure salaries and those with lesser incomes, between the 'ideal types' who are heirs to family fortunes and those who are not, between those who hold substantial portfolios of shares and those who only dabble in the stock market, between those who live in mansions and those who live in more routine detached houses, between those who read only the *Financial Times* and those who read the *Guardian*, between those

who went to public school and those who went to a state comprehensive, and so on. Of course, the absolute 'ideal types' may not, in
reality, exist at all. Nevertheless, a holistic approach will take
account of all possible permutations of past, present and, so far
as possible, future circumstances to produce a more finely gradated
class hierarchy that can accommodate the vast majority of individuals more comfortably than the existing framework. To be
accurate, it will have more than the five or six tiers of the traditional
classifications; to be meaningful, it will – at any one time – segment a
population of 58 million into a limited number of groups in a clearly
defined pecking order.

This book recognises the ascendancy and expansion of the middle
classes, and the triumph of the values they hold dear. It heralds a
more self-confident individualism, as well as a shift towards a more
open, fluid and meritocratic society. A new generation has grown to
maturity on a diet of individual aspiration, self-improvement and
the right to acquisitiveness; the inherited superiority of the upper
classes is in decay and the old solidity of the industrial working
classes has been atomised. The ranks of the middle classes are
swollen by newcomers, both the upwardly mobile and the downwardly mobile. To pretend class does not exist is akin to not
recognising the inescapable variables of race or gender: that some
people are black and some are white, that some are male and some
female. Although class is not genetically determined, it would still
exist even if class prejudice were to be abolished. It arises out of a
recognition that groups of individuals have common characteristics
that result in similar behaviour, which in turn reinforces common
characteristics. It cannot be otherwise, except in a society of robots –
and, even then, only if all the robots are of the same model. The
crucial question is not whether class still exists, but what is the
nature of the new class structure.

In the next chapter a simple questionnaire aims at measuring the
material, behavioural, attitudinal and aspirational elements that
combine to distinguish you as an individual, with a specific past,
present and future that determine the direction of your class
mobility. It is tailored to reveal where you stand in the pecking
order, what sets you apart as well as what you have in common with
other individuals who share a similar class position. The approach is
distinctive and rests on the belief that in a predominantly middle-
class society your lifestyle, in the broadest sense of the word,

distinguishes your social ranking rather than the other way round. The three-dimensional approach reveals the dynamics of your class position, whether you are moving upwards, downwards or remaining stagnant. It also leaves it up to you – not the whim of market researchers – to decide whether your class position is dependent on that of somebody else, such as a husband, wife or partner. With the questionnaire, just as with income tax, you can choose to be treated as a freestanding individual and answer accordingly, or as one half of a couple, taking the circumstances of both people into account. The middle-class revolution is not played out yet, but out of the chaos and uncertainty of its after-shock is emerging a reformation, not abolition, of class. The underlying message is that you can influence, even determine and change, your class. It is not immutably fixed by the rest of society. As Margaret Thatcher, who rightly claimed to have 'changed everything', said in a much-misunderstood and much-distorted reference: 'There is no such thing as society. There are individual men and women, and there are families . . . and people must look to themselves first.'

CHAPTER TWO
——

QUESTIONS OF CLASS

NOBODY need be a lifelong prisoner of the class they were born into. As we will show, where you are in the social pecking order of the 1990s does not depend simply on who your parents were, where you were educated, what you do for a living, or even how much you earn.

The three-dimensional approach to class means your past is important but not oppressive, your present is crucial but always changing, and your future is shaped by ambition as much as fate. What you buy is as significant as how much you spend; what you know counts as much as which school you went to; and your taste in cars, clothes and culture can set you apart more than 'breeding' ever could.

But class is a perpetual game of snakes and ladders. When you answer our 60 questions, remember the game is full of ups and downs. Your position is constantly changing or maturing. Age can play a part and young people frequently spend a period in limbo, occupying an ill-defined or particularly ephemeral class position as they grow to full adulthood and learn to exercise their own individuality.

Complete the questionnaire below, which will take no more than about 30 minutes. After you have ticked your answers, find out what your answers say about you by reading the following chapters on the importance of your beginnings, your education, your wealth, your home, your car and your career. You can discover how you have fared by adding the marks on the scoresheet in Appendix I to calculate exactly where you stand in today's social hierarchy, and to find out whether you are going up or down, or merely treading water. Remember to be as honest as you can: you will fool nobody but yourself!

THE DO-IT-YOURSELF TEST TO DISCOVER WHERE
YOU ARE IN THE NEW SOCIAL PECKING ORDER

1. More than ever before, personal wealth is a powerful indicator of where you stand in society. What you earn is the starting point for securing a foothold on the class ladder. What is your annual income before tax? (*Tick one*)

   (a) More than £100,000   _____
   (b) £50,001–£100,000   _____
   (c) £32,001–£50,000   _____
   (d) £22,001–£32,000   _____
   (e) £16,001–£22,000   _____
   (f) £11,001–£16,000   _____
   (g) £8,001–£11,000   _____
   (h) £8,000 or less   _____

2. How much you expect your annual earnings to increase is a measure of your ambition and self-confidence. Which is the closest estimate to how you think your earnings will change, in cash terms, over the next five years? (*Tick one*)

   (a) At least treble   _____
   (b) Double   _____
   (c) Increase by about half   _____
   (d) Increase by about a third   _____
   (e) Increase by about a tenth   _____
   (f) Neither increase nor decrease _____
   (g) Decrease   _____

3. Some people, however, sacrifice earnings for the trappings of success. What are the perks of your current job?

   (a) Business expense account   _____
   (b) Company car   _____
   (c) Company pension   _____
   (d) Free or subsidised holidays   _____
   (e) Free or subsidised meals   _____
   (f) Free or subsidised personal travel _____
   (g) Free or subsidised products   _____
   (h) Medical insurance   _____

    (i)   Mobile phone   _____
    (j)   School fees for children   _____
    (k)   Subsidised mortgage   _____
    (l)   Any other perks   _____
    (m)   No perks   _____

4.   Where you keep your cash is a clue to what kind of earner
you are. A Coutts account has more clout than one with the
Co-op. Where is your main account? (*Tick one*)

    (a)   Abbey National   _____
    (b)   Allied Irish Banks   _____
    (c)   Bank of Ireland   _____
    (d)   Bank of Scotland   _____
    (e)   Barclays   _____
    (f)   Child & Co   _____
    (g)   Clydesdale   _____
    (h)   Co-operative   _____
    (i)   Coutts & Co   _____
    (j)   First Direct   _____
    (k)   Girobank   _____
    (l)   Hoare   _____
    (m)   Lloyds   _____
    (n)   Midland   _____
    (o)   NatWest   _____
    (p)   Royal Bank of Scotland   _____
    (q)   TSB   _____
    (r)   Ulster Bank   _____
    (s)   Yorkshire Bank   _____
    (t)   Any other bank   _____
    (u)   Any building society   _____
    (v)   No bank or building society account _____

5.   Everyone tries to save for a rainy day, but only the better-off
succeed. How much do you have in your savings accounts?
(*Tick one*)

    (a)   More than £25,000   _____
    (b)   £10,001–£25,000   _____
    (c)   £5,001–£10,000   _____

    (d) £1,001–£5,000   _____
    (e) £301–£1,000   _____
    (f) £1–£300   _____
    (g) None   _____

6. The credit boom has made it possible for millions of people to spend today and pay tomorrow. Your credit rating is a benchmark of your financial status. What is the total limit of all the credit and charge cards that you can draw on? (*Tick one*)

    (a) More than £20,000   _____
    (b) £10,001–£20,000   _____
    (c) £3,001–£10,000   _____
    (d) £1,401–£3,000   _____
    (e) £751–£1,400   _____
    (f) Up to £750   _____
    (g) No credit or charge cards   _____

7. Stocks and shares are no longer the preserve of a wealthy élite. The share-owning democracy has eroded the divisions of the them-and-us culture. What is the estimated market value of the shares you own? (*Tick one*)

    (a) More than £30,000   _____
    (b) £10,001–£30,000   _____
    (c) £5,001–£10,000   _____
    (d) £1,001–£5,000   _____
    (e) £301–£1,000   _____
    (f) £1–£300   _____
    (g) No shares   _____

8. Inheritance is the new class liberator. The post-war explosion in home-ownership means today's younger generation stand to come into a fortune. What is the value of money and property you have already inherited? (*Tick one*)

    (a) £500,001 or more   _____
    (b) £200,001–£500,000   _____
    (c) £100,001–£200,000   _____

(d) £50,001–£100,000 _____
(e) £5,001–£50,000 _____
(f) £1–£5,000 _____
(g) None _____

9. At current prices, what is the value of money and property you expect to inherit? (*Tick one*)

(a) £500,001 or more _____
(b) £200,001–£500,000 _____
(c) £100,001–£200,000 _____
(d) £50,001–£100,000 _____
(e) £5,001–£50,000 _____
(f) £1–£5,000 _____
(g) None _____

10. Whether you are a City stockbroker or a primary school teacher, your job helps establish your place in the social hierarchy. Which group of jobs in Appendix II contains the one nearest to your own (Groups A–F)?

_____

11. None of us can escape our past. What your parents do, or did, for a living can either open doors or keep them shut. Which group in Appendix II contains the job nearest to the highest-paid occupation of either of your parents (Groups A–F)?

_____

12. For most people, the benchmark of success is whether they are better off than their parents. Overall, how much wealthier or poorer are you than your parents? (*Tick one*)

(a) A lot wealthier _____
(b) A little wealthier _____
(c) Neither wealthier nor poorer _____
(d) A little poorer _____
(e) A lot poorer _____

13. What is the minimum that your annual earnings will have to be before you regard yourself as wealthy? (*Tick one*)

(a) More than £1 million _____
(b) £500,001–£1 million _____

(c) £250,001–£500,000   _____
(d) £100,001–£250,000   _____
(e) £75,001–£100,000   _____
(f) £50,001–£75,000   _____
(g) £35,001–£50,000   _____
(h) £20,001–£35,000   _____

14. Your formative years define your outlook and influence your ambition. There is no denying that standards of education in the private sector have generally surpassed those in the state system. What sort of primary or preparatory school(s) did you attend? (*Tick one*)

(a) Private   _____
(b) State   _____
(c) Both   _____

15. What sort of secondary school(s) were you educated at? (*Tick one*)

(a) Direct-grant grammar   _____
(b) Fee-paying independent   _____
(c) State comprehensive   _____
(d) State grammar   _____
(e) State secondary modern   _____
(f) Mixture of independent and state _____

16. Many millionaires left school at 16; for others, the age they left is a shameful secret. When did you leave school? (*Tick one*)

(a) Before 16   _____
(b) 16 or 17   _____
(c) 18 or above   _____

17. Higher education is a passport to class improvement. Where did you go after school?

(a) Ancient university other than
         Oxbridge   _____
(b) Art school   _____

31

(c) Britannia Royal Naval College,
     Dartmouth   _____
(d) Catering college   _____
(e) Further education college   _____
(f) Harvard Business School   _____
(g) Any other business school   _____
(h) Hendon Police College   _____
(i) Higher education college   _____
(j) Lucie Clayton college   _____
(k) Oxbridge   _____
(l) Secretarial college   _____
(m) Polytechnic or 'new' university   _____
(n) RADA   _____
(o) Redbrick or 'plate-glass' university   _____
(p) Royal Agricultural College,
     Cirencester   _____
(q) Any other agricultural college   _____
(r) Royal Air Force College, Cranwell   _____
(s) Royal College of Music   _____
(t) Royal Military Academy, Sandhurst   _____
(u) Sorbonne   _____
(v) Any other foreign university   _____
(w) Swiss finishing school   _____
(x) Teacher training college   _____
(y) Other institution   _____
(z) No education or training after
     school   _____

18. Do you have a degree or an equivalent qualification?

    (a) Yes   _____
    (b) No   _____

19. Where your parents were educated can be an inhibiting
    embarrassment if you want to get on. What sort of schools
    did your father attend? (*Tick one*)

    (a) Fee-paying independent   _____
    (b) State   _____
    (c) Mixture of independent and state   _____

20. And your mother? (*Tick one*)

    (a) Fee-paying independent   _____
    (b) State   _____
    (c) Mixture of independent and state   _____

21. Which of your parents attended university? (*Tick one*)

    (a) Both   _____
    (b) One   _____
    (c) None   _____

22. The kind of home you live in is one of the most defining statements of class pretensions. Which of the following most closely describes your main home? (*Tick one*)

    (a) Bedsit   _____
    (b) Bungalow   _____
    (c) Country house   _____
    (d) Detached house   _____
    (e) Farmhouse   _____
    (f) Flat/maisonette   _____
    (g) Mansion   _____
    (h) Penthouse or similar apartment   _____
    (i) Semi-detached house   _____
    (j) Terraced house   _____

23. A Georgian house is more desirable than a contemporary modern home. When was your main home built? (*Tick one*)

    (a) Pre-Georgian   _____
    (b) Georgian   _____
    (c) Victorian   _____
    (d) Edwardian   _____
    (e) 1918–1939   _____
    (f) 1940–1959   _____
    (g) 1960–1989   _____
    (h) 1990 onwards   _____

33

24. You can never say you have made it until you have got a place of your own. Do you: (*Tick one*)

    (a) Own your home   _____
    (b) Rent from a council   _____
    (c) Rent from a private landlord   _____
    (d) Own a home you bought from a council
           under right-to-buy legislation   _____

25. The big question then becomes: how much is your main home worth? (*Tick one*)

    (a) More than £1 million   _____
    (b) £320,001–£1 million   _____
    (c) £160,001–£320,000   _____
    (d) £120,001–£160,000   _____
    (e) £88,001–£120,000   _____
    (f) £68,001–£88,000   _____
    (g) £52,001–£68,000   _____
    (h) £40,001–£52,000   _____
    (i) Up to £40,000   _____
    (j) Not a home-owner   _____

26. Size matters. How many bedrooms does your main home have? (*Tick one*)

    (a) Five or more   _____
    (b) Four   _____
    (c) Three   _____
    (d) Two   _____
    (e) One   _____
    (f) Bedsit   _____

27. How many bathrooms? (*Tick one*)

    (a) Three or more   _____
    (b) Two   _____
    (c) One   _____
    (d) None   _____

28. What size is your garden? (*Tick one*)

(a) More than five acres _____
(b) Between one and five acres _____
(c) Half an acre _____
(d) One third of an acre _____
(e) 100ft by 30ft _____
(f) 50ft by 30ft _____
(g) Small patio garden _____
(h) Roof garden or terrace _____
(i) Shared garden _____
(j) Only a backyard _____
(k) No garden or backyard _____

29. The icing on the cake will be the cars parked outside. How many cars have you got? (*Tick one*)

(a) Three or more _____
(b) Two _____
(c) One _____
(d) None _____

30. The type of car you drive is crucial for making your mark. What is the current value of the most expensive car you drive? (*Tick one*)

(a) More than £25,000 _____
(b) £15,001–£25,000 _____
(c) £10,001–£15,000 _____
(d) £7,501–£10,000 _____
(e) £5,001–£7,500 _____
(f) £2,500–£5,000 _____
(g) Less than £2,500 _____
(h) No car _____

31. You can quickly fall behind on the class escalator if you do not maintain a full complement of material possessions. Which of the following do you own?

(a) Burglar alarm _____
(b) Cable television _____

35

(c) Camcorder _____
(d) Compact disc player _____
(e) Dishwasher _____
(f) Electronic personal organiser _____
(g) Élite or personalised car registration _____
(h) Grand piano _____
(i) Horse _____
(j) Jacuzzi _____
(k) Mobile telephone _____
(l) More than £1,000 of silver or
      porcelain china _____
(m) Painting or sculpture worth more
      than £1,000 _____
(n) Personal computer _____
(o) Rolex or Cartier watch _____
(p) Satellite television _____
(q) Sauna _____
(r) Second car _____
(s) Second home abroad _____
(t) Second home in the United Kingdom_____
(u) Swimming pool _____
(v) Tennis court _____
(w) Timeshare _____
(x) Video recorder _____
(y) Yacht _____
(z) None of these _____

32. The days of *Upstairs, Downstairs* are gone. However, the upwardly mobile increasingly require the services of others. Do you employ or have you recently employed:

(a) An au pair _____
(b) A butler or maid _____
(c) A chauffeur _____
(d) A childminder _____
(e) A cleaner _____
(f) A cook _____
(g) A gardener _____
(h) A gillie _____
(i) A nanny _____

(j)   A private nurse   _____
(k)   A private tutor for your children   _____
(l)   None of these   _____

Your precise position in the pecking order can depend on awareness of cultural icons, and knowledge of who and what really counts. Your class ranking can come down to the 'airs and graces' you adopt as well as the words you say, the films you watch and the newspapers you read.

33.   Which daily newspaper do you read? (*Tick one*)

(a)   *Daily Express*   _____
(b)   *Daily Mail*   _____
(c)   *Daily Mirror*   _____
(d)   *Daily Sport*   _____
(e)   *Daily Star*   _____
(f)   *Daily Telegraph*   _____
(g)   *Financial Times*   _____
(h)   *Glasgow Herald*   _____
(i)   *Guardian*   _____
(j)   *Independent*   _____
(k)   *International Herald Tribune*   _____
(l)   *Irish Independent*   _____
(m) *Irish Press*   _____
(n)   *Irish Times*   _____
(o)   *Morning Star*   _____
(p)   Regional daily newspaper   _____
(q)   *Scotsman*   _____
(r)   *Sun*   _____
(s)   *The Times*   _____
(t)   *Today*   _____
(u)   *Wall Street Journal*   _____
(v)   None of these   _____

34.   Which Sunday newspaper do you read? (*Tick one*)

(a)   *Independent on Sunday*   _____
(b)   *Mail on Sunday*   _____
(c)   *News of the World*   _____
(d)   *Observer*   _____
(e)   *People*   _____

(f) *Scotland on Sunday*   _____
(g) *Sunday Express*   _____
(h) *Sunday Independent*   _____
(i) *Sunday Mirror*   _____
(j) *Sunday Sport*   _____
(k) *Sunday Telegraph*   _____
(l) *Sunday Times*   _____
(m) *Sunday Tribune*   _____
(n) None of these   _____

35. Every television channel has its own identity. Which one do you watch the most? (*Tick one*)

(a) BBC 1   _____
(b) BBC 2   _____
(c) Channel Four   _____
(d) ITV   _____
(e) Satellite movie channels   _____
(f) Satellite shopping channel   _____
(g) Sky News   _____
(h) Sky One   _____
(i) Radio Telefis Eireann   _____
(j) Other   _____
(k) Do not watch television   _____

36. Radio listeners are more discriminating. Which station do you listen to the most? (*Tick one*)

(a) Radio One   _____
(b) Radio Two   _____
(c) Radio Three   _____
(d) Radio Four   _____
(e) Radio Five Live   _____
(f) Classic FM   _____
(g) World Service   _____
(h) Independent local radio   _____
(i) BBC local radio   _____
(j) Other   _____
(k) Do not listen to the radio   _____

37. You are branded by where you shop. Which store are you or
     your family most likely to visit for your main food shopping?
     (*Tick one*)

     (a) Asda   _____
     (b) Co-op   _____
     (c) Costco or other discount
          clubs   _____
     (d) Delicatessen   _____
     (e) Fortnum & Mason   _____
     (f) Gateway/Somerfield   _____
     (g) Happy Shopper   _____
     (h) Harrods Food Halls   _____
     (i) Kwiksave   _____
     (j) Local shop   _____
     (k) Market stalls   _____
     (l) Marks & Spencer   _____
     (m) Morrisons   _____
     (n) Safeway   _____
     (o) Sainsbury   _____
     (p) Shoprite   _____
     (q) Tesco   _____
     (r) Waitrose   _____
     (s) Wm Low   _____
     (t) Other stores   _____

38. From which two are you most likely to buy your clothes?
     (*Tick no more than two*)

     (a) BhS   _____
     (b) Burtons   _____
     (c) C&A   _____
     (d) Clery's   _____
     (e) Debenhams   _____
     (f) Miss Selfridge   _____
     (g) Dressmaker   _____
     (h) Freemans or other similar
          mail-order catalogues   _____
     (i) Harrods   _____
     (j) Harvey Nichols   _____

(k) House of Fraser or similar
       department store   _____
(l) Independent shop or boutique   _____
(m) Jenners   _____
(n) John Lewis   _____
(o) Laura Ashley   _____
(p) Liberty   _____
(q) Littlewoods   _____
(r) Marks & Spencer   _____
(s) Next   _____
(t) Oasis   _____
(u) River Island   _____
(v) Switzers   _____
(w) Tailor   _____
(x) The Gap   _____
(y) Top Man/Top Shop   _____
(z) None of these   _____

You are what you wear. Which two items of clothing would you most like to wear? (*Tick no more than two*)

39. For men:

(a) An Armani suit   _____
(b) An Austin Reed suit   _____
(c) Anything by Top Man   _____
(d) A Barbour   _____
(e) A Burberry raincoat   _____
(f) Corduroy trousers   _____
(g) A Gieves & Hawkes suit   _____
(h) A leather bomber jacket   _____
(i) A Marks & Spencer suit   _____
(j) A nylon quilted driving coat   _____
(k) A pair of chinos   _____
(l) A Pierre Cardin shirt   _____
(m) A shellsuit   _____
(n) A Turnbull & Asser shirt   _____
(o) An Yves St Laurent suit   _____
(p) None of these   _____

40. For women:

(a) An Aquascutum raincoat _____
(b) A Barbour _____
(c) Anything from C&A _____
(d) A Caroline Charles two-piece suit _____
(e) A Chanel two-piece suit _____
(f) A Dorothy Perkins blouse _____
(g) A French Connection dress _____
(h) A fur coat or jacket _____
(i) A Hermes scarf _____
(j) A Laura Ashley dress _____
(k) Leggings _____
(l) A Marks & Spencer two-piece suit _____
(m) A shellsuit _____
(n) A velour sweatshirt _____
(o) A Versace blouse _____
(p) None of these _____

41. What you do in your spare time reinforces your class position. Do you attend, watch or take part in:

(a) Ballet _____
(b) Bingo _____
(c) Bridge _____
(d) Casino gambling _____
(e) Cricket _____
(f) Golf _____
(g) Greyhound racing _____
(h) Horse-racing _____
(i) Hunting _____
(j) Opera _____
(k) Pigeon-fancying _____
(l) Point-to-point _____
(m) Polo _____
(n) Riding _____
(o) Rugby League _____
(p) Rugby Union _____
(q) Sailing _____
(r) Scuba-diving _____

(s) Shooting   _____
(t) Skiing   _____
(u) Snooker   _____
(v) Soccer   _____
(w) Squash   _____
(x) Tennis   _____
(y) Theatre   _____
(z) None of these   _____

42. The social calendar is for everyone. Which two of the
     following events would you most like to attend? (*Tick no
     more than two*)

(a) All-England tennis championships
        at Wimbledon   _____
(b) Badminton Horse Trials   _____
(c) The Edinburgh Festival   _____
(d) The National Eisteddfod   _____
(e) Rugby international at Twickenham _____
(f) The Epsom Derby   _____
(g) The FA Cup Final   _____
(h) Glyndebourne   _____
(i) The Grand National   _____
(j) The greyhound derby at Wimbledon _____
(k) A grouse moor on the Glorious
        Twelfth   _____
(l) Henley Regatta   _____
(m) Last Night of the Proms   _____
(n) Another Proms concert   _____
(o) A May Ball at an Oxbridge college _____
(p) The Oxford and Cambridge
        Boat Race   _____
(q) A pheasant shoot   _____
(r) Royal Ascot   _____
(s) The Rugby League Cup Final   _____
(t) Rugby international at Murrayfield _____
(u) A Test Match at Lord's   _____
(v) Rugby international at Cardiff
        Arms Park   _____

(w) The West End premier of a Lloyd
       Webber musical   _____
(x) The World Snooker Championships
       at Sheffield   _____
(y) A Knebworth rock festival   _____
(z) The World Darts Championship   _____

43. Which are your two favourite drinks? (*Tick no more than two*)

(a) Baileys   _____
(b) Bitter   _____
(c) Blended whisky   _____
(d) Cappucino   _____
(e) Champagne   _____
(f) Claret   _____
(g) Darjeeling tea   _____
(h) Earl Grey tea   _____
(i) Espresso   _____
(j) Gin and tonic   _____
(k) Gold Blend instant coffee   _____
(l) Guinness or other stout   _____
(m) Harvey Wallbanger   _____
(n) Lager   _____
(o) Lager and lime   _____
(p) Liebfraumilch   _____
(q) Mineral water   _____
(r) PG Tips   _____
(s) Port   _____
(t) Port and lemon   _____
(u) Real ale   _____
(v) Sherry   _____
(w) Single malt whisky   _____
(x) Vermouth   _____
(y) Vodka and tonic   _____
(z) None of these   _____

44. If you were to dine out for pleasure only once a week, how
     much of your own money would you be most likely to spend
     on a meal for two? (*Tick one*)

(a) £200 at a Michelin-starred restaurant _____

43

(b)   £100 at a country house hotel   _____

(c)   £70 at a French restaurant   _____

(d)   £30 at an Italian restaurant   _____

(e)   £30 at a tapas bar   _____

(f)   £25 at a country pub   _____

(g)   £20 at a Chinese or Indian
      restaurant   _____

(h)   £20 at a steak house   _____

(i)   £10 at McDonald's   _____

(j)   £5 at a fish-and-chip shop   _____

(k)   None of these   _____

45.   Which one of the following holidays would you prefer?
      (*Tick one*)

(a)   Golf in the Algarve   _____

(b)   Holiday village in Bermuda   _____

(c)   A coach trip to Bulgaria   _____

(d)   A shopping weekend to Calais
      hypermarkets   _____

(e)   Stay with friends in California   _____

(f)   Skiing in Aspen, Colorado   _____

(g)   A hotel on the Costa del Sol   _____

(h)   A week at a Center Parc resort in
      England   _____

(i)   A trip to Walt Disney World in
      Florida   _____

(j)   Caravanning in Holland   _____

(k)   A guided tour of Renaissance Italy   _____

(l)   A *gîte* in the Loire Valley   _____

(m)   Diving off the Maldives   _____

(n)   Shopping trip to New York   _____

(o)   A cruise around the eastern
      Mediterranean   _____

(p)   Walking in the Pyrenees   _____

(q)   Winter sun in Tenerife   _____

(r)   Topless bathing on Pattaya beach,
      Thailand   _____

(s)   Sightseeing in Vietnam   _____

(t)   None of these   _____

46. Role-models are important. We all have heroes who help articulate our class ambitions. Actors, authors and prominent figures in public life hold the biggest sway. Which two contemporary male film stars do you most admire? (*Tick no more than two*)

(a) Warren Beatty   _____
(b) Kenneth Branagh   _____
(c) Michael Caine   _____
(d) Tom Cruise   _____
(e) Bob Hoskins   _____
(f) Jeremy Irons   _____
(g) Daniel Day-Lewis   _____
(h) Robert de Niro   _____
(i) Gerard Depardieu   _____
(j) Michael Douglas   _____
(k) Clint Eastwood   _____
(l) Harrison Ford   _____
(m) Arnold Schwarzenegger   _____
(n) Sylvester Stallone   _____
(o) Robin Williams   _____
(p) Bruce Willis   _____
(q) None of these   _____

47. And female? (*Tick no more than two*)

(a) Helena Bonham Carter   _____
(b) Pauline Collins   _____
(c) Joan Collins   _____
(d) Jodie Foster   _____
(e) Goldie Hawn   _____
(f) Holly Hunter   _____
(g) Emily Lloyd   _____
(h) Dolly Parton   _____
(i) Vanessa Redgrave   _____
(j) Miranda Richardson   _____
(k) Julia Roberts   _____
(l) Sharon Stone   _____
(m) Emma Thompson   _____
(n) Madonna   _____

(o) Julie Walters   _____
(p) Sigourney Weaver   _____
(q) None of these   _____

48. Which three authors are you most likely to read? (*Tick no more than three*)

(a) Margaret Atwood   _____
(b) Julian Barnes   _____
(c) Anita Brookner   _____
(d) Julie Burchill   _____
(e) Tom Clancy   _____
(f) Jackie Collins   _____
(g) Catherine Cookson   _____
(h) Jilly Cooper   _____
(i) Colin Dexter   _____
(j) Roddy Doyle   _____
(k) Ben Elton   _____
(l) Frederick Forsyth   _____
(m) P.D. James   _____
(n) Stephen King   _____
(o) Colleen McCullough   _____
(p) Terry Pratchett   _____
(q) Salman Rushdie   _____
(r) Tom Sharpe   _____
(s) Joanna Trollope   _____
(t) Fay Weldon   _____
(u) None of these   _____

49. When or where do you most frequently read novels? (*Tick one*)

(a) In bed   _____
(b) On holiday   _____
(c) At home in the evening   _____
(d) On trains or buses   _____
(e) At weekends   _____
(f) Never   _____

50. Which two British men do you most admire? (*Tick no more than two*)

    (a) Paddy Ashdown   _____

    (b) Lord (Richard) Attenborough   _____

    (c) Tony Benn   _____

    (d) Richard Branson   _____

    (e) Archbishop of Canterbury   _____

    (f) Chris Evans   _____

    (g) Sir Ranulph Fiennes   _____

    (h) Paul Gascoigne   _____

    (i) Douglas Hurd   _____

    (j) Gary Lineker   _____

    (k) John Major   _____

    (l) Nigel Mansell   _____

    (m) John McCarthy   _____

    (n) Lord Tebbit   _____

    (o) Prince of Wales   _____

    (p) Terry Waite   _____

    (q) None of these   _____

51. And female? (*Tick no more than two*)

    (a) Kate Adie   _____

    (b) Cilla Black   _____

    (c) Naomi Campbell   _____

    (d) Sally Gunnell   _____

    (e) Felicity Kendall   _____

    (f) Glenys Kinnock   _____

    (g) Joanna Lumley   _____

    (h) Norma Major   _____

    (i) Jill Morrell   _____

    (j) The Queen   _____

    (k) The Queen Mother   _____

    (l) Esther Rantzen   _____

    (m) Anita Roddick   _____

    (n) Margaret Thatcher   _____

    (o) Princess of Wales   _____

    (p) Mary Whitehouse   _____

    (q) None of these   _____

52. What's in a name? From Abigail to Winston, what you call
your children is imbued with class connotations. Which of
the following do you like most as a first name for a son?
(*Tick one*)

(a)   Adam   _____
(b)   Alexander   _____
(c)   Ashley   _____
(d)   Charles   _____
(e)   Christopher   _____
(f)   Craig   _____
(g)   Daniel   _____
(h)   Darren   _____
(i)   Darryl   _____
(j)   Edward   _____
(k)   George   _____
(l)   Henry   _____
(m)   James   _____
(n)   Jason   _____
(o)   Justin   _____
(p)   Lee   _____
(q)   Matthew   _____
(r)   Max   _____
(s)   Michael   _____
(t)   Nicholas   _____
(u)   Oliver   _____
(v)   Robert   _____
(w)   Ryan   _____
(x)   Samuel   _____
(y)   Thomas   _____
(z)   William   _____

53. And for a daughter? (*Tick one*)

(a)   Alexandra   _____
(b)   Alice   _____
(c)   Amy   _____
(d)   Camilla   _____
(e)   Charlotte   _____
(f)   Dawn   _____

48

(g) Eleanor   _____
(h) Elizabeth   _____
(i) Emily   _____
(j) Emma   _____
(k) Fay   _____
(l) Georgina   _____
(m) Hannah   _____
(n) Harriet   _____
(o) Jessica   _____
(p) Katherine   _____
(q) Kelly   _____
(r) Kylie   _____
(s) Lucy   _____
(t) Olivia   _____
(u) Rachel   _____
(v) Rebecca   _____
(w) Sarah   _____
(x) Sharon   _____
(y) Sophie   _____
(z) Tracy   _____

54. Which two activities would you most like a child of yours to pursue? (*Tick no more than two*)

(a) Ballet   _____
(b) Boxing   _____
(c) Boys' Brigade   _____
(d) Cricket   _____
(e) Disco dancing   _____
(f) Golf   _____
(g) Highland dancing   _____
(h) Karate or judo   _____
(i) Majorettes   _____
(j) Montessori schooling   _____
(k) Philately   _____
(l) Playing computer games   _____
(m) Playing a musical instrument _____
(n) Rudolf Steiner schooling   _____
(o) Scouts or Guides   _____
(p) Soccer   _____

(q) Weight-training   _____
(r) Woodcraft Folk   _____
(s) None of these   _____

55. Accents have never had more cachet. The Queen's English is under siege and vocabulary is no longer a crucial class indicator. On occasions, however, you still have to watch your language. Which one of the following words or phrases do you most commonly use? (*Tick one*)

(a) Bathroom   _____
(b) Bog   _____
(c) Lavatory   _____
(d) Loo   _____
(e) Privy   _____
(f) The smallest room in the house   _____
(g) Toilet   _____
(h) WC   _____
(i) None of these   _____

56. And: (*Tick one*)

(a) Couch   _____
(b) Settee   _____
(c) Sofa   _____
(d) None of these   _____

57. And: (*Tick one*)

(a) Afters   _____
(b) Dessert   _____
(c) Pudding   _____
(d) Sweet   _____
(e) None of these   _____

58. What do you call the main evening meal? (*Tick one*)

(a) Dinner   _____
(b) High tea   _____
(c) Supper   _____

(d) Tea   _____
(e) None of these   _____

59. Where do you relax at home? (*Tick one*)

(a) In the back room   _____
(b) In the drawing room   _____
(c) In the kitchen   _____
(d) In the living room   _____
(e) In the lounge   _____
(f) In the sitting room   _____
(g) None of these   _____

60. How far are you prepared to go? What have you done to
     improve your class position?

(a) Disowned your parents   _____
(b) Faked academic qualifications   _____
(c) Falsified your curriculum vitae   _____
(d) Lied about your family background   _____
(e) Name-dropped people you barely
       know   _____
(f) Paid for elocution lessons   _____
(g) Sent children to private school even
       though you always said it was
       against your principles   _____
(h) None of these   _____

CHAPTER THREE

BEGINNINGS

*T*HE three-dimensional approach to class recognises the social legacy we all inherit from our parents, our upbringing and the values that are inculcated from the moment we are born. Unlike traditional classifications, it does not pretend that we ever entirely escape the environment that nurtured us in our most formative years. Neither does it accept eugenic or hereditarian arguments about class being passed down the generations as if it were genetically determined that you are born to be of a particular class. However, the seeds of your own social classification – separate from that of your parents – are sown even before the first day of your life. The clues are there in black and white on the birth certificate: your name, where you were born, and what your parents do for a living. Even at the register office your parents can find themselves being asked whether, in the course of their work, they supervise 'other employees'.

It used to be the rule that the class you were born into was the class you died in. From the cradle to the grave, your family background was always with you, whether as a help or a hindrance. It is different now: in itself, your background only vaguely foreshadows rather than determines your subsequent class position. Whereas previously you carried your class origins throughout your life, fewer and fewer vestiges of your background now encumber you. You cannot choose or change the distant past of childhood; it is not like the immediate past of adulthood, which is, of course, only yesterday's present. Although there is no hard and fast rule, your family background is important mainly insofar as it either inspires or dampens class ambition. It provides the launchpad for your own class journey. You can begin to carve out a new class identity, separate from that of your parents, as soon as you take your first step outside the family home. Parents who went to public school and university may set a higher benchmark against which to strive than parents who left state school at 14; wealthy parents, who provided an early comfortable environment in which to grow, may also offer the security that comes with the prospect of a certain financial inheritance in later life. Neither, however, is without pitfalls that can nurture complacency and stagnation: it is no coincidence that so many middle-class children are 'a disappointment' to their parents. Brought up often without the competitive instinct or desire for self-improvement of those lower in the social hierarchy, they can easily find themselves slipping down the class ladder.

In signifying your class position, your parentage is far less important than how you behave as a parent. These days parents are propelling their offspring into society at ever earlier ages, handing them into the care of nannies, child-minders or simply friends, ferrying them back and forth to Tumbletots, registering them for 'mornings only' at the Montessori on the other side of town, or even just sitting them in front of the goods on offer in the commercials between children's television programmes. For many parents, their children are an articulation of their own class position, in much the same way as a house or car is. Parents bask in the reflected glory that parenthood brings.

A name is the first thing all parents give their children, and it can leave a lasting imprint of a baby's class beginnings; it also serves as marker of parental aspirations. 'What's in a name?' asked Shakespeare's Juliet. She should have asked Kylie and Darren, or Tracey and Trevor, and Sharon and Wayne. Or Harriet and Oliver, and Abigail and Alexander, and Georgina and Nicholas. Your name is an echo from your past; the name you give your children is a much more immediate clue to your present and the future you envisage for your offspring. As a rule, ambitious parents choose a name they think is favoured by people in a slightly higher social class, even when their role-models exist only in an Australian soap. Imagine two girls playing in the broken-down lift of a council tower block in a northern industrial city: it is unthinkable that one of them should be called Camilla. Conversely, imagine two young boys marching off the playing fields of Eton: it is equally inconceivable that one should be called Duane. Marshall McLuhan wrote: 'The name of a man is a numbing blow from which he never recovers.' Onomastics (the study of names) has established that many have distinct class associations, and that what you are called can influence how others regard you or treat you.

Fashions change over the generations and the favourite of today's élite can become common o' garden within a decade; the reverse can also be true. Some names are notably ambivalent, depending on the era in which they are chosen and the reasons for which they are favoured. Take Kevin, for example: Kevin Keegan – distinctly plebeian; Kevin Costner or Kline – far more culturally refined because of their Hollywood associations. The name Abigail once became so closely associated with ladies' maids that it almost disappeared, only to be taken up later by the middle classes. So the Sharons and Traceys who became synonymous with Essex in the 1980s may find themselves reborn in more exclusive circles in the 21st century. However, the names with real social cachet in new generations are revealed only when those generations come to maturity and you start noticing how common or uncommon some names are, and who has them. It is a mysterious process: the Bible, the Royal Family, literature, film stars and, latterly, soap stars are some of the most common sources that inspire people of different classes. Traditional 'classless' favourites from the Old Testament – rather than the New Testament – are enjoying something of a renaissance among a middle class that cannot countenance the idea of naming their children after contemporary royals. Charles, Diana, William, Andrew and even Camilla do not command automatic popularity. Instead, aspiring parents are more likely to seek inspiration for 'Christian' names from the Romans or the Greeks, from pagan times, from the Celtic strand or, if from royalty, from a period when the monarchy was held in higher regard. Hence the nostalgia for names such as Victoria, Charlotte, Edgar and Oswald; it cannot be long before Albert makes a reappearance. Alistair, Fergus, Feargal and Liam also have a certain social exclusivity.

Sometimes the choice is influenced by everyday experience, by subconsciously copying the admirable and avoiding the detestable: the naughty girl at playgroup, who is called such-and-such, 'but what can you expect with that sort of mother?'; the sweet little so-and-so who always does so well at school, 'and from *such* a nice family, too!' So how are upwardly mobile parents to know which ones to choose? The most authoritative guide is provided by the personal columns of *The Times*. In 1993, Alexander and Sophie were the first names most frequently chosen by families wanting to advertise the arrival of a baby in the traditional showcase for middle-class parenthood. Studies have shown that the names most popular with readers of *The Times* are significantly different from those favoured by the masses; they have also indicated, though, that the ones that figure in *The Times*'s top 10 are a pointer to those that will be among the most popular overall in a decade a more. Alexander has only narrowly edged Thomas into second place, followed by James, the most popular boys' name of all over the past 30 years. The gap is even closer among the girls, where fashions are more volatile. Sophie had a fight on her hands to head off a challenge from Olivia, one of the most upwardly mobile names of the last few years, though she has yet to gain much of a foothold outside the middle classes; her success may yet be reinforced by newspaper headlines about Sophie Rhys-Jones, the public relations consultant who became Prince Edward's girlfriend.

The findings are based on a study of the first names of more than 4,000 babies sharing 349 boys' names and 488 girls' names; some of the more eccentric choices included Cloudy, Quinta and the typographically challenged Atalanta. A separate analysis of names registered throughout England and Wales has Daniel and Rebecca as the most popular choices, accounting for one in 23 of all first names. One of the most intriguing undercurrents in *The Times*'s list is the apparent impact of royalty and the Queen's 'annus horribilis' of 1992. Camilla, a household name since rumours surrounding Camilla Parker Bowles's relationships with the Prince of Wales, edged towards the top 10, with 24 mentions, making it more popular than either Rachel or Sarah; the name of Diana was advertised only once in *The Times*.

Among boys, the top 10 – including eight Old Testament names and accounting for more than one third of all boys' births announced in the newspaper – have been filled by only a dozen names in the past five years. Samuel, which entered the lists in 1990 and 1991, appears to have peaked; Robert, tenth in 1988 and 1989, has still to make a reappearance. Oliver, in ninth place in 1993, was at its lowest ebb for five years, while Edward continued to struggle in seventh position and was on the verge of being overtaken by Henry. Nicholas, a new arrival in 1992, clung on to tenth spot.

For girls, competition is even keener for a place in the top 10: a total of 16 names have figured in *The Times*'s list since 1988. The most significant absentees of 1993 were Alexandra and Hannah, both prominent in the previous year's rankings; other top choices to have made it in the past but failed in 1993 were Sarah (seventh in 1991), Jessica (eighth in 1990), and Katherine (seventh in 1988 and eighth in 1989). After a three-year absence, Elizabeth re-emerged in ninth position in 1993. For Eleanor, it was the first time she had earned a top spot in five years. Researchers have traced the beginnings of her mass appeal to 'Eleanor Rigby', the Beatles' song of 1966.

However, the most remarkable phenomenon is that of Olivia, a name that gained prominence in the birth columns in 1989. Four years later, it was the first preference for one in 35 of all girls named in *The Times*, compared with only one in 238 in the country as a whole. Only two of the top boys' names in *The Times* – Thomas and James – also appear in the list of the 10 most popular names overall; according to this list, Alexander is 18th, followed by William (25th), Nicholas (29th), Oliver (33rd), Edward (41st), and Charles (44th). George and Henry, whose popularity outside a narrow élite has generally waned since the war, do not even make the overall top 50. Girls' names reveal a similar class bias: only Charlotte and Emma feature in both top 10s. Overall, Emily is 13th, followed by Sophie (14th), Alice (44th), Lucy (20th), Elizabeth (32nd) and Eleanor (40th). Olivia and Georgina do not feature in the overall top 50. Evidence about the most favoured middle-class names is confirmed by readers' choices in the *Daily Telegraph*. The favourites are remarkably similar to those in *The Times*, except, for girls, Rebecca and Alexandra figured towards the bottom of a top 10 in which there was no place for Elizabeth, Georgina or Harriet; for boys, the only difference was that *Telegraph* readers favoured Jack but not Nicholas.

THE MOST POPULAR NAMES IN 1993

Girls

The Times	**Overall**
1. Sophie (1)	1. Rebecca (5)
2. Olivia (4)	2. Charlotte (–)
3. Emily (3)	3. Laura (4)
4. Alice (8=)	4. Amy (–)
5. Charlotte (2)	5. Emma (3)
6. Eleanor (–)	6. Jessica (–)
7. Lucy (5)	7. Lauren (–)
8. Emma (–)	8. Sarah (1)
9. Elizabeth (–)	9. Rachel (7)
10.= Georgina (8=)	10. Catherine (–)
10.= Harriet (7)	

Boys

The Times	**Overall**
1. Alexander (3)	1. Daniel (5)
2. Thomas (1)	2. Matthew (2)
3. James (2)	3. James (4)
4. William (4)	4. Christopher (1)
5. Charles (7)	5. Thomas (–)
6. George (6)	6. Joshua (–)
7.= Henry (9)	7. Adam (–)
7.= Edward (8)	8. Michael (8)
9. Oliver (5)	9. Luke (–)
10.= Nicholas (10)	10. Andrew (6)

Source: *The Times* birth announcements of 1993, and *The Guinness Book of Names*, 1993 for overall listings. Figures in brackets refer to top 10 positions in 1992 for *The Times* and 1985 for the overall listings for England and Wales.

Inevitably, variations in the most common names can be identified across the regions. An analysis of 12,000 new-born babies photographed by Parasol Portrait Photography, a Surrey-based company, confirmed the pre-eminence of Daniel and Rebecca, but pointed to Scott as the most popular boys' choice in Scotland, and James in southeast England in 1993. For girls, regional favourites included Charlotte in London, Rebecca and Claire in Scotland, Laura in southeast England, and Emma in Wales. However, Leslie Dunkling, author of *The Guinness Book of Names*, says it is *The Times* that generally foreshadows the coming favourites among the masses. 'Some of these names are definitely on the way up. Up to 10 years after names appear in *The Times* they become far more popular in the country as a whole,' he says. 'Parents get a feeling that they are the kind of choice liked by people in the class slightly above. They are not simply copied, but seep slowly into the national consciousness.' Consequently, it is safe to assume that 1993 finally sealed the fate of Trevor and Kevin, who received only one mention each. Darren, Tracey and Sharon failed to register a single entry.

THE MOST POPULAR NAMES THIS CENTURY

Boys				
1900	**1950**	**1975**	**1985**	**1993**
1. William	David	Stephen	Christopher	Daniel
2. John	John	Mark	Matthew	Matthew
3. George	Peter	Paul	David	James
4. Thomas	Michael	Andrew	James	Christopher
5. Charles	Alan	David	Daniel	Thomas
6. Frederick	Robert	Richard	Andrew	Joshua
7. Arthur	Stephen	Matthew	Steven	Adam
8. James	Paul	Daniel	Michael	Michael
9. Albert	Brian	Christopher	Mark	Luke
10. Ernest	Graham	Darren	Paul	Andrew

Girls				
1900	**1950**	**1975**	**1985**	**1993**
1. Florence	Susan	Claire	Sarah	Rebecca
2. Mary	Linda	Sarah	Claire	Charlotte
3. Alice	Christine	Nicola	Emma	Laura
4. Annie	Margaret	Emma	Laura	Amy
5. Elsie	Carol	Joanne	Rebecca	Emma
6. Edith	Jennifer	Helen	Gemma	Jessica
7. Elizabeth	Janet	Rachel	Rachel	Lauren
8. Doris	Patricia	Lisa	Kelly	Sarah
9.= Dorothy	Barbara	Rebecca	Victoria	Rachel
9.= Ethel				
10.	Ann	Karen	Katherine	Catherine
		Michelle		

Source: *The Guinness Book of Names*, 1993.

Names are only the starting point. The class differences in how parents set about bringing up their children are as stark as in any other aspect of life. For the babies born in John Major's 'classless' Britain, the pigeon-holing begins from the moment they open their eyes. Will they see the pastel colours of a private room in the Portland Hospital in central London, thanks to parental contributions to an expensive medical insurance scheme, or will they be sharing an NHS ward, all peeling paintwork and scuffed linoleum, with at least three other new-borns? Will they find themselves in their parents' bedroom, one of a growing number of home births made fashionable again by the middle classes? Or will they be coming up for air after surviving the novelty of a water birth, the tub paid for on their parents' World Wide Fund for Nature affinity credit card? Out in the street the social differences are easy to spot. Increasingly, children are mascots of parents keen to advertise their class position. From baptism outfits to baby Barbours, the clothes they wear are just as much class statements as fashion statements. One toddler, the offspring of an aspirational couple, sports the latest Oshkosh striped dungarees, imported from the United States and with a £30 price tag. On its feet are a pair of German-made multi-coloured boots costing £35, width and length selected by a trained shoe-fitter. Another toddler is less fortunate: she wears a garish tracksuit from BhS, price £12.99, and walks around in Mothercare trainers costing £9.99, chosen for size by her mother.

Nowhere are the upwardly mobile more aspirational than in their desire for pre-school education, a multi-million-pound industry that has mushroomed since the mid-1980s with the growth of private nurseries and special classes to cater for toddler 'hobbies', from ballet and gymnastics to tennis and learning French. Some parents have gone so far as to put down the names of their children for public school while they were still foetuses in the womb. In the age of 'designer babies', parental engineering has replaced social engineering by the State. Successful parents have assumed responsibility for ensuring their children get a better start in life. No longer can they rely on the State to do their job for them. The vacuum of pre-school provision by the State has enabled middle-class parents to use their money to steal a march on the rest.

It is a crucial distinction: the middle classes invest in the future of their children, while the working classes spoil them in the here and now. Middle-class couples pay up to £3,000 a year to ensure that children as young as two get the 'solid grounding' they need to secure a place at the best independent schools. They recognise the importance of nurturing the potential of their offspring rather than satisfying their immediate needs. The working classes, by contrast, can be seen every weekend traipsing round Toys 'Я' Us, their shopping trolleys stuffed with Thunderbirds replicas, Barbie dolls, the latest computer games and more. A child's electric motor car costing up to £500, equivalent to a term's fees at a private nursery school, is regarded as money well spent. Unlike the middle classes, who expect their offspring to become high achievers from an early age, the respectable working classes are content to see their children behave themselves and not 'go off the rails'. In the subterranean world of the underclass, however, single parents struggle even to provide a stable family life. A latch-key culture is emerging in which children as young as three are left to fend for themselves. The upper classes, meanwhile, are having to take a more direct interest in their children's upbringing. It is no longer sufficient to produce a son and heir and then rely on a nanny and a top public school to bring him to his majority. Inheritance is no longer the certainty it was, and for the first time the children of the aristocracy are learning workaday skills to prepare for the worst: having to go out and get a job. So pervasive are middle-class values that it is socially unacceptable to grow up simply as one of the 'idle' rich.

Parenthood in the 1990s is increasingly about what you can do for your children rather than the personal relationship you have with them. Middle-class couples can be as cold and unfeeling as the worst 'Home Alone' single mothers to hit the tabloid headlines. The main difference, though, is that they can provide the best beginnings that money can buy, shuffling off their parental duties on to an army of surrogate carers. They make it possible for their children to get a head start by providing access to the widest range of pre-school education. The 1993 *Good Nursery Guide* feeds on this new middle-class obsession. It describes more than 300 top schools for toddlers, most of which specialise in preparing pupils for entry to the prep schools that will eventually lead to senior schools such as Eton and Roedean. Pooh Corner Montessori School in Kensington, west London, 'aims to give a child the best possible chance to beat the hot competition for places in London's élite private schools'. Parents are warned that 'children must be potty-trained before starting' but are assured they will be 'capable of addition and

subtraction up to 10' by the time they are five. Fees at that time were
£1,800 a year, mornings only.

At Winchester House Pre-Prep Nursery in Brackley, North-
amptonshire, children are 'carefully groomed for the public school
system' from the age of three, and progress is monitored daily.
Three-year-olds hoping for a place at a top nursery in Leeds are
interviewed and 'assessed for maturity, ability to listen and con-
centrate, language and comprehension, observancy and readiness';
two in three are rejected. One of the most expensive establishments
listed in the guide is Holland Park Nursery School in west London,
charging £3,500. Babies can start at three months; stripped down to
their nappies, they begin with finger-painting, known as 'structured
free play'. Nearly all the nurseries have long waiting lists. To stand
any chance of getting a place at some of them, parents are advised to
plan child care 'well ahead of birth'.

Montessori schools are the academic hothouses used by children
of aspiring middle-class parents. In fact, this could not be further
from what Maria Montessori, Italy's first woman doctor of
medicine, intended when she developed her approach in the early
years of this century from her work with deprived and neglected
children in the slums of Rome. Her aim was to encourage children to
become free-thinking, independent learners. Montessori education
in Britain, however, is almost exclusively restricted to middle-class
children, whose families can afford – or are prepared to spend
between £500 and £900 on fees every term. There is an added
bonus: having a child at a Montessori school is a status symbol in its
own right and eases the conscience of parents who have their own
lives to lead.

Lower down the social scale, Britain faces a childcare crisis as
more mothers than ever enter the workforce. State nurseries
currently have places for only one child in 100, a situation that is
unlikely to improve over the next few years, despite John Major's
ambitions to provide pre-school education for all. Child-minding is
by far the most popular form of paid child care: there are now more
than 100,000 child minders registered with local authorities, looking
after 300,000 children and paid between £40 and £90 a week. But
having to use a child minder is being forced to accept second best:
'dumping' your child in someone else's home, often with other
children, puts them at the mercy of someone else's lifestyle and
influence.

Nevertheless, the nanny state is truly upon us. Once the preserve of the upper classes, nannies are hired by working couples in good jobs who plan their daily schedules at home and at work around myriad commitments contained in their Filofaxes and electronic personal organisers. They are a far cry from Mary Poppins and the Edwardian governess, the sort of people who pursue 'careers' and are no longer inspired by a sense of vocation. There are an estimated 35,000 nannies in Britain, looking after children in their own homes. Unlike child minders, they do not come cheap: the average weekly earnings for a living-out nanny are more than £180, and even when accommodation is included, they gross an average of £130.

Au pairs, preferably Nordic or Spanish students, are a cut-price and much-favoured alternative. They offer many of the advantages of nannies: they are always at hand in your home, available for babysitting and ready to fit in with your working hours. They will even clean, shop and iron – and all for as little as £35 a week plus bed and board. What used to be a hallmark of a small and wealthy élite is trickling down the social order to become a more widely available commodity among the ordinarily prosperous who previously would not have had the space to accommodate paid help. It is, of course, important not to let friends or neighbours think you are exploiting vulnerable young foreigners

For many members of the new élite, the ultimate achievement is to have the best of both worlds: to have a successful career but not one that impinges on their ability to be a diligent parent. Not everybody has to spend 12 hours a day in the office to do their job: working from home and 'tele-commuting' are ideal for ambitious parents. It is no accident that Richard Branson, the Virgin tycoon, holds executive meetings in his own west London home.

The big question is to what extent are family ties important? A three-dimensional approach to class recognises the importance of your early years in setting the tone for where you see yourself in society. By the age of seven, it is said, children are on their way to becoming independent individuals capable of drawing their own conclusions about their likes and dislikes. That is why Ignatius Loyola, the 17th-century Jesuit philosopher, adopted the maxim: 'Give me a boy of seven and he is ours for life.' Any older and the child would know its own mind.

The influence of family background, however, is weakening. The class position of today's adults is less dependent on their upbringing than that of previous generations; when today's children grow up, their beginnings will seem even more remote. One reason is the changing importance of parents: they are no longer the sole role-models for impressionable youth, and many are barely role-models at all. Far from wanting to end up like their parents, children yearn to make their own mark in the world. By the time they are teenagers, many are so divorced from the family home that they use it as if it were a hotel or their own personal fast-food restaurant. Children are no longer constrained by their mothers' apron-strings. The number of women at work in Britain has grown by more than 1 million since the mid-1980s and it is estimated that up to two-thirds of mothers are now in a job, or looking for work; almost half have children under school age. Of the 7 million mothers with children at home, over 1 million are single parents. With more disposable income and far greater expectations than past generations, working parents devote as much time to their own careers and leisure activities as to their children. The talk these days is of 'quality time' spent with their offspring, the child-rearing equivalent of a television or radio 'sound-bite'.

In the media age, parents cannot compete with the plethora of instant heroes. They began the losing battle as long ago as the 1960s when the ration-book generation was supplanted by baby-boomers nurtured in a climate of affluence. The emergence of youth culture – typified by The Who's pop anthem 'My Generation' and the immortal line 'Hope I die before I get old' – has played a crucial part. In the days of Elvis Presley and the Rolling Stones, children went out of their way to rebel against their parents. Since then, it has become routine for them to look outside the home for role-models they have never even seen in the flesh: from pop icons to sporting heroes, American superstar wrestlers and even computer-generated characters who exist only within arcade games. It was only to be expected. Parents brought up in the 'permissive society' of the 1960s have permitted their children to go their own way. They see it as a duty to encourage them to decide for themselves who to imitate. At the same time, children have become disillusioned with their parents: for every two marriages in Britain in 1991 there was one divorce, often resulting in acrimonious court battles over family finances and custody. They instinctively ask whether they want to be like their fathers and mothers: nearly one in five unmarried adults is cohabiting. The people they want to impress are not their parents, but members of their own generation, many of whose class origins are far different from their own.

Children are no longer only appendages fashioned in the image of their parents. From an early age, they are committed consumers and active members of society. With pocket money as much as £100 a month, they are targets of advertisers keen to exploit the buying habits of the young. By the age of four they are already hooked on the social significance of having the 'right' material possessions, whether it is a Sonic the Hedgehog computer game or a replica of the latest Manchester United football strip, a Swedish-made Brio wooden train set or something from the new Early Learning Centre catalogue. They are mini class warriors with their own building society and bank accounts: nearly one in three put aside their pocket money in savings, according to research by Walls', the food manufacturer.

The loosening of parental ties has proved a bonus for some, a disadvantage for others. The greatest benefit has been to free aspirational individuals upwards. Gone are the days when parents at the lower end of the social scale expect their children to pursue the same mundane, dirty jobs that were good enough for them, their own parents and their parents' parents. Among the upper classes there is a gradual trend towards encouraging their offspring to stand on their own two feet, particularly those who are not in direct line to succeed to an aristocratic title. They, too, are becoming more middle class: 'breeding' is less about pedigree – whether your family was here before the Norman Conquest and what sort of blood runs in your veins – and more about preparedness to adapt to the present.

The true importance of modern parents is as providers. The main thing they provide is opportunity and choice, and not just those that can be bought by money alone. Nepotism, the scourge of the meritocracy, still prevails at all levels of society. It can wangle you a job as a docker or a postman, or a career as a high-flying merchant banker or journalist. The circle of friends and acquaintances enjoyed by your parents can open doors that remain tightly shut to the less privileged. Of course, the higher up the social scale you are to begin with, the more options you are given. But how far you then progress up the class ladder depends on you. Your parents may give you a good start in life, but the goals you set yourself and the lifestyle you choose will be derived from all the influences that bear down on you outside the family home. Your background can either help or hinder, but it can never serve as an adequate excuse for under-achievement. When it comes to class, ultimately you are on your own.

CHAPTER FOUR

*S*CHOOL TIES

'*E*TON or Winchester, old boy?' is a question that typified the assumptions of the old upper class. Now, in the boardrooms of Britain and the corridors of Whitehall, the response could just as well be, 'Birmingham, actually'. Where you go to school is the starting point for becoming aware of the social class you were born into. For the upwardly mobile it can be an early liberator from a humdrum background. Before the age of five, you are cocooned in a world so small that it is only when you leave it that you discover it was not unique. You find there are hundreds like you, whether they are the nannied rich of the public schools, the working-class successes of the grammar schools, or the second-class denizens of the secondary moderns. You literally learn to feel 'at home' with others like you, and alien from those who are different. Your education can embed you in your class, it can start to free you from it, or it can even drag you down. The three-dimensional view of class recognises that your education is an enduring foundation of your ultimate position in society and one that influences the choices you make later in life. Whatever career you subsequently pursue, it cannot be ignored as a weighty ingredient of your social status. Throughout adulthood, the school or university you and even your parents went to – or did not go to – will crop up time and again as part of the 'baggage' you carry, both in your own eyes and in the eyes of others. Similarly, the school or university you send your children to will influence how others regard you.

The education system is a mirror image of the class system. The undercurrents of social change swirl to the surface in the type of schools we choose for our children. Inevitably, it affects how our own educational career is viewed: if you are in your late 30s or 40s, to have gone to a state grammar is today a badge of meritocratic achievement. However, the phenomenon of the past decade has been the expansion of private schools to meet the demands of the flourishing middle classes, whose members have traditionally rejected the state system of mass education, with its overcrowded classes, dog-eared textbooks, lack of discipline and dilatory pursuit of individual excellence. Two separate developments, however, have coincided to transform the social make-up of many 'posh' public schools and further dilute the strength of the old upper classes: the abolition of direct-grant grammar schools in the early 1970s, and the ability and enthusiasm of a rising number of aspiring 'first-time buyers' – those who have no family tradition of private schooling – to pay for their children's education. Often, one parent in a couple goes out to work simply to pay for the education of their children: schooling is just another service in a consumer society. The engulfing spread of comprehensives put many middle-class, and even working-class, parents on the spot. For them, it marked the end of a golden age of free state schooling that gave their children a chance to attend either direct-grant grammars modelled directly on the best of the independent sector, or state-run grammars that enjoyed only slightly inferior status. Thereafter, the state system was too hit-and-miss to satisfy the expectations of the aspiring middle classes, of whom only a fortunate and tiny minority could count on their children going to a well-run state school with an impressive head-teacher and outstanding academic achievements.

As the comprehensive revolution added a political dimension to the private-versus-state argument, middle-class parents were forced to settle on one side or the other of the divide. In the 1980s, with Thatcherism fuelling the growth of upwardly mobile consumers, the proportion of children attending independent schools increased from less than 6% to nearly 8%. For the cost of a second car, family holidays abroad or a slightly bigger mortgage, education has become another item for consumer choice rather than a totem of old-fashioned class habit. More people want it and more people are able to afford it. No longer is it sufficient to make the crude distinction between 'upper-class' private schools and the rest for the rest. The middle classes have won the day, and paying a fortune in school fees has replaced having to leave it to the state to provide. Like a Trojan horse, the middle classes, laying siege to the institutions that harboured the old élite, are camped out at the heart of the mushrooming public school system.

State schools, even comprehensives, can have attractions in prosperous catchment areas, where selection according to ability has been replaced by selection according to size of mortgage. But even there, parents have no guarantee that paying an extra £10,000 or more for houses near a better school will get the standard of education they want for their children. Within a culture of state mediocrity there has been a confusing and uncertain assortment of methods of classifying pupils: the old 11-plus in a handful of areas where grammars survive; streaming by ability in comprehensives; setting by ability in different lessons; and while a few schools have sought to stretch the most able children, most are still wedded to a so-called egalitarian approach that levels down the most able children rather than levers up the rest. For the middle classes, schooling is a risky business: if their children mix with the wrong sort – and that often includes the teachers – they could find themselves downwardly mobile almost from the start.

The state system is finally trying to make up lost ground by trying to become as diverse and success-oriented as the independent sector. Free-market changes within state education are enabling more parents to exercise choice not only between different schools, but also between different types of schools. Publication of examination results and the introduction of national curriculum tests have allowed them to make more informed choices. Out of all this are emerging national and local 'league tables', with scores of state schools capable of competing in the premier division with many of the best private schools. Just as there is an increasing overlap between the types of families using the two sectors, so there is an inter-mingling of the schools themselves and how they compare. The average private school still has higher status than the average state primary or secondary; the average grammar has higher status than the average comprehensive; and the aspiring grant-maintained schools are forging a higher status than council-run counterparts. And yet, each of these statements conceals important truths: the best state school, for example, can outstrip the average private school and the best comprehensive can rival a run-of-the-mill grammar school. In education, as in other parts of life, the gap between the best and worst is widening, with best becoming a much more heterogeneous élite.

In higher education, Oxbridge still dominates. But it is not the Oxbridge of *Brideshead Revisited* or *The Glittering Prizes*. The upper-class bias of both ancient universities has been enervated by the meritocratic impetus in the real world beyond the ivory towers. For example, in 1963 half the undergraduates entering Oxford came from independent schools, just over a third came from state-maintained schools, and the rest (15%) were from direct-grant grammars; at the end of the 1960s and after the expansion of higher education, the proportions of pupils from independent and state-maintained schools were roughly equal at just over four in 10 each, while the proportion from direct-grant grammars remained broadly the same (17%). However, by the late 1970s – at the very end of the state system's golden age – the state-maintained schools, predominantly grammars, had pulled ahead, all this in a period when the number of students at Oxford also increased markedly. It is only with the abolition of direct-grant schools, the spread of comprehensives and the subsequent expansion of private education that the balance has swung back, marginally, in favour of independent schools. Never has the background of Oxbridge students, regardless of the type of school they attended, been less upper class.

A degree used to be so impressive that letters after your name marked you out as someone of standing. Today, only the most desperate to impress would contemplate boasting that they were a BA or BSc; and only ageing headteachers would be sufficiently proud of being a BEd to put it on a school board. There has been a revolution in higher education, with the number of students doubling to 1.3 million since 1970. The proportion of people with degrees, or their equivalent, has increased sharply in the past decade, from 9% to 12% for men, and from 4% to 7% for women. Expansion of university places is the 'big bang' of middle-class ascendancy. In future, if you are not a graduate, you will find yourself out on a limb. But within the world of higher and further education there are new hierarchies and fresh choices, between the old universities and the 'new' universities, between the 'in' colleges and the rest. As choice in education expands, so do the opportunities for establishing and asserting your social advancement.

Disenchantment with the state sector is most severe among the new middle-class parents who contrast today's state system with their own post-war experiences, largely as pupils at grammar schools. A clear majority of parents (54%) now choosing to send their children to private schools were educated exclusively in the state system; the proportion has increased sharply, from 41%, in four years; only a quarter of parents comprise couples who both attended private school. Moreover, about half of all private-school parents, even those who fit the classic stereotype, have considered sending their children to a state school, and a quarter have children in both sectors. However, frustration with the 'poor' quality of state education is quoted by more than a quarter of parents as a reason for choosing private schools, while one in three believes that money buys a better standard of education. As with pre-school education, parental engineering is replacing state-run social engineering. Most significantly, three in 10 parents going private are manual or clerical workers outside occupational groups A and B; and as many as one in 25 comes from the C2s, Ds and Es. There is plenty of evidence to suggest that many others have been put off only because of the recession and rising school fees, which have increased by nearly half since 1989 and can now exceed £12,000 a year. It is too early to say whether or not government reforms in the state system will be enough to turn the tide, but one thing is certain: there is nothing public, in the routine sense of the word, about public schools.

THE MOST EXPENSIVE PRIVATE SCHOOLS

	Annual Fees
Westminster, central London	£12,750
Millfield, Somerset	£12,435
Harrow, outer London	£12,360
Winchester, Hampshire	£12,270
Bryanston, Dorset	£12,255
Oundle, Northamptonshire	£12,021
Roedean, East Sussex	£11,985
Eton, Berkshire	£11,934
Cobham Hall, Kent	£11,922
Charterhouse, Surrey	£11,910
Bedales, Hampshire	£11,901
Rugby, Warwickshire	£11,865
Uppingham, Leicestershire	£11,850
King's, Canterbury	£11,820
St Edmund's, Canterbury	£11,820
Tonbridge, Kent	£11,820
Haileybury, Hertfordshire	£11,775
Benenden, Kent	£11,730
Stowe, Buckinghamshire	£11,730
Sherborne, Dorset	£11,700

Source: Independent Schools Information Service 1993.

Having children at private school is a powerful symbol of wealth and aspiration. The proportion of private pupils from families earning more than £40,000 a year now constitutes a clear majority, having increased by half since 1989; however, even though the recession has taken its toll, more than four in 10 earn less than £40,000 a year, while one in seven earns less than half that; about 29,000 children are helped under the Assisted Places Scheme aimed primarily at parents with an annual income of less than £34,000. David Woodhead, director of the Independent Schools Information Service, is confident there has been a far-reaching change in the kind of children who now attend fee-paying schools, one in 13 of all pupils compared with one in 20 in the 1970s. 'Clearly the independent sector isn't some kind of hermetically sealed system or a no-go area for all but an exclusive and self-perpetuating class,' he says. Undoubtedly, when the economy picks up again, even more of the clerical workers, middle managers and other beneficiaries of the 1980s' boom will once again opt for independent education. The cultural wall between the state and private sectors will continue to be much more permeable than at any time in the past.

WHO SENDS THEIR CHILDREN TO PRIVATE SCHOOL?

Occupational group	%
A	22
B	41
C1	26
C2	3
DE	1

Source: Independent Schools Information Service/MORI, 1994.

Even within the self-selecting minority who opt for private education, there are clear signs of social diversity beyond the simple measure of wealth and earnings. While quality newspapers such as *The Times*, the *Daily Telegraph* and the *Financial Times* are all read by between 20% and 30% of private-school parents, there are many tabloid-reading families who also send their sons and daughters to fee-paying schools: more than one in five (21%) is a regular reader of the *Daily Mail* and about one in 10 (9%) is a *Daily Express* reader. Although six in 10 private-school parents are, unsurprisingly,

listeners to BBC Radio 4, one in six is a regular listener to BBC
Radio 1, the same proportion as for BBC Radio 2; only one in seven
(14%) tunes in to BBC Radio 3.

It is easy to be misled into thinking that nothing much has changed.
The popular image of public schools – the sort of people who
attended them, the attitudes they have and the privileges they enjoy
– is buttressed by evidence that is, in reality, up to 50 years out of
date. The old-boy network that holds sway in the top echelons of
politics, commerce and the bureaucracy is populated by men, and a
few women, who were young more than a generation ago. As a
result, the schools and universities they went to will not necessarily
be the ones that produce the successful class warriors of the future:
many schools live on slow-fading glory. Others are the same schools
in name only: the sort of pupils attending them and the parents
patronising them are very different. A generation ago, the educational divides were as sharp and uncomplicated as the divisions in
society as a whole: the private schools led by their own élite of Eton,
Harrow, Roedean and the rest; the state grammar schools headed by
their direct-grant cousins, which served the old middle class as well
as the cream of the academic and aspiring working class; and the
secondary moderns for the industrial working class and sundry
no-hopers or no-chancers. *The Official Sloane Ranger Handbook*
summed up the importance of public schools in grooming the old
élite in surroundings of suitable grandeur: 'If you spend approximately 10 years of your life in a very large house with its own chapel,
in a closed society where the Cabinet and heads of the armed forces
are just ahead of you – Old Boys or Girls – you identify with the
powerful. Gothic suits you: you feel physically at home in Law
Courts or the Houses of Parliament or the pavilion at Lords. You see
yourself as a small person in a huge hall where history is being made.
You may be small, but you share in the great enterprise. Sloanes put
tradition top because it keeps them top.' Similarly, in higher
education, Oxbridge – with its dreaming spires, punts and May
Balls – and a handful of other ancient universities had it all to
themselves.
    Although the 1944 Education Act has wreaked fundamental
change in the subterranean depths of the class system, only now
are the effects of the post-war expansion of education beginning to
be seen at the top of society, where the stranglehold of an exclusive

circle of public schools, within the wider exclusion zone of private education, is starting to loosen. Symbolically, the last five prime ministers, spanning a period of 30 years and following a trio of Etonians, have all been state-educated, most notably John Major, who left Rutlish Grammar in southwest London at 16 with, famously, no O-levels. 'Never has so much been said about so little,' he recalled after winning the Tory party leadership battle with Douglas Hurd, the first Conservative politician to find that being an Etonian, scholar and a gentleman was actually a disadvantage; in vain Hurd tried to portray himself as the horny-handed son of a humble farmer. Curiously, no such problems confronted Michael Heseltine, Major's other rival and an alumnus of Shrewsbury School; his wealth, though, is that of a self-made businessman. Even Heseltine, however, was not without his critics: Alan Clark, the former trade minister and millionaire whose home is Saltwood Castle in Kent but whose grandfather was a cotton king, once said sniffily that his party colleague not only couldn't shoot straight, but he even bought his own furniture!

The spirit of meritocratic change is finally enabling the men and, perhaps more remarkably, women who attended grammar schools in the 1950s, as well as many of the 'minor' public schools, to push aside the remnants of a generation whose main qualifications were a large family purse, an old school tie and personal knowledge of people who mattered, often relatives or friends. The new and emerging élite, therefore, come from a greater number of more meritocratic schools; some even attended the 'redbrick' or 'plate-glass' universities that have revamped the pecking order since the expansion of higher education in the early 1960s. They are eating away at the Establishment's educational and social prejudices, adding momentum to the changes of which they are a part, and defining a new order of schools and universities.

It is, of course, possible to find evidence to support claims that the old school tie still has the nation in its noose. At the end of 1992 the *Economist* analysed the backgrounds of '100 top people'. They were overwhelmingly male; two-thirds went to public school; more than half went to Oxbridge. The magazine compared the results with the same exercise conducted 20 years earlier. There were minor changes: the average age had dropped, from 58 to 57; the number of women had doubled, from two to four; the proportion who went to public school had fallen by a single percentage point, from 67% to

66%; within the public schools, a wider range was represented after Eton's share dropped from one in seven (14%) to one in 12 (8%). The proportion of those who had not enjoyed some form of higher education had halved.

In Whitehall the picture is the same. The 1992 *Whitehall Companion*, a collection of biographies of nearly 1,000 senior civil servants, revealed just how far John Major's 'classless' Britain has yet to go to penetrate corridors of power still populated by members of an Oxbridge 'mafia' educated at expensive public schools: more than half of those in the highest echelons of government studied at Oxford or Cambridge; in some departments Oxbridge people held two in three of the most senior posts; eight of the 12 biggest government departments were run by permanent secretaries – none of them women, all of them white – who had Oxbridge degrees and attended fee-paying schools. The Treasury had the strongest Oxbridge bias, with seven in 10 of those in the top four civil service grades having attended the two ancient universities; in second place was the Department of Trade and Industry, with 38 of its 54 senior officials having been to Oxbridge. Ironically, it was the Treasury that probably had the most senior and notable 'class migrant' in its permanent secretary, Sir Terence Burns, who attended Houghton-le-Spring Grammar School and Manchester University.

Consequently, by studying the backgrounds of many at the top of society, it may appear that only modest progress has been made towards a more meritocratic class structure and that its pace has been snail-like. It is, perhaps, not too surprising given the size, dominance and formidable history of the old Establishment. Even so, there are clear signs that the pace is accelerating, in a process spurred by the Thatcher years but coming to fruition only in the decade after she left office. The shock waves will continue well into the 21st century as 'Thatcher's children' grow to adulthood. Already, there is substantial evidence that social shifts among the mass of the population are starting to bubble to the surface and intrude into the rarefied atmosphere of the ruling Establishment.

Take a look at the 1993 *Who's Who*, the 145th edition of the annual biographical dictionary of 'the great and the good': 29,000 politicians, civil servants, business people, academics, artists, aristocrats and local government bureaucrats. 'An invitation to appear in *Who's Who* has, on occasion, been thought of as conferring distinction,' says a preface by the unnamed editor. 'That is the last thing it can do. It recognises distinction and influence.' The modern-day bible of the Establishment offers a snapshot of those in power and those crossing the threshold of power; about half its invitations are issued automatically, to new MPs, judges, barristers and civil servants. The secret committee that meets throughout the year to consider nominations attempts to reflect changes in the Establishment and opinion-formers' views of it. Typically, the only way you can leave the authorised version of the Establishment is if you die; it has been estimated that your chances of getting your name in are 75 times greater if your father was in it. In 1993 some 900 people made their début in *Who's Who* and 700-plus, whose entries first appeared a generation ago, departed because they had died in the previous 12 months. What can we learn about the academic and social background of the emerging Establishment compared with that of the old guard? While a comparison reveals how the educational currents of the past 30 years have yet to overturn the established order – Oxbridge and the old élite of Eton, Winchester and Harrow remain the surest passport to a *Who's Who* entry – it does show that people from public schools previously dismissed as 'minor', as well as those from state grammars, are beginning to break through.

The comparison between the 'old guard' and the *Who's Who* newcomers shows there has been a notable decline in the influence of top public schools: one in three of the emerging Establishment in 1993 was educated privately, compared with half of the 'old guard'. Eton remains the most successful Establishment kindergarten, though it, too, has lost ground: overall, in the 1993 *Who's Who*, there were 1,245 Etonians, just over one in 25 of all entries and five times the number of Harrovians; in 1963 the proportion of Etonians was more than one in 20 and less than four times the number of Harrovians. Of the 'old guard' members whose entries were removed because they had died before publication of the 1993 edition, 390 were schooled in the independent sector; the biggest number had gone to Eton and Winchester. A total of 126 had attended the 13 most-represented public schools. A similar dilution in the influence of Oxbridge can also be detected: among the new entries, about a quarter (27%) studied at either Oxford or Cambridge, compared with more than a third (34%) of the departing Establishment. Trinity, Cambridge, and New College, Oxford, remain the colleges with a direct route into the corridors of power.

WHERE THE OLD GUARD WAS EDUCATED

Public schools	Universities
Eton (41)	Cambridge (133)
Winchester (16)	Oxford (118)
Harrow (13)	London (23)
Clifton College (10)	Wales (8)
Marlborough (9)	Liverpool (8)
Wellington (9)	Edinburgh (7)
Westminster (6)	Durham (7)
Stowe (6)	Glasgow (6)
Charterhouse (5)	Queen's, Belfast (5)
Dulwich (5)	Manchester (5)

Source: *Who's Who* obituary list, 1993; out of 700 entries.

. . . AND THE *WHO'S WHO* NEWCOMERS

Public schools	Universities
Eton (21)	Oxford (142)
Winchester (9)	Cambridge (99)
Marlborough (8)	London (55)
Sherborne (7)	Glasgow (20)
Charterhouse (6)	Edinburgh (20)
Clifton College (6)	Bristol (18)
Westminster (6)	Durham (16)
Cheltenham College (5)	Manchester (16)
Bradford Grammar (5)	Leeds (11)
King's Canterbury (5)	Birmingham (10)

Source: *Who's Who*, 1993; out of 900 new entrants from school or university.

For the class-conscious cognoscenti, it is not enough simply to say Oxford or Cambridge. Even within the educational élite, there are pecking orders. The Norrington Table, which ranked Oxford colleges according to their degree results, used to be the academic equivalent of a snob's guide that created an inner élite of educationally respectable institutions. It was proof positive that Merton, New College and St John's were 'in', while St Peter's, Somerville and Trinity were definitely 'out'. But the distinctions between the colleges go further than mere degree performance: they all have their own social niches. Balliol thrived on its reputation for the 'effortless superiority' of intellectual left-wingers; Christ Church, all beagling and bun-fights at Piers Gaveston Society dinners, is the preserve of the landed gentry who refer to it simply as 'The House'; Oriel is perhaps best known for its beefy American rowers, who enjoy their 15 minutes of fame in the annual Boat Race.

The most remarkable characteristic of today's élite, however, is not the high proportion of members who are Etonians, Harrovians or Oxbridge types, the seeds of which were, after all sown in the Victorian era. It is the way the grip of the old school tie, the badge of an outdated aristocracy, is being broken by the success of Britain's 'minor' public schools and the jewels in the crown of the state system. When the *Financial Times*, the house newspaper of the ruling élite for more than a century, surveyed 50 independent school headmasters, Oxbridge tutors and A-level examiners, it revealed a shake-up of seismic proportions in the long-established hierarchy of private education. It showed that the rising élite is likely to come from fee-paying schools with a reputation for academic achievement rather than blind social snobbery. There was room in the top 10 for only four of the 'great' public schools listed by the 1861 Clarendon Commission, including Eton, Winchester, Harrow, Westminster, St Paul's, Charterhouse, Merchant Taylor's, Rugby and Shrewsbury. There was only passing mention of Charterhouse, which was damned by the faint praise of one headmaster. 'It tends to be dominated,' he opined, 'by stock-brokers' sons. It leads to a certain moral climate.'

Top of the boys' rankings was King Edward's, Birmingham, a former direct-grant grammar whose 'old boys' include Sir Michael Checkland, former director-general of the BBC; Sir Peter Walters, former chairman of Midland Bank, who describes his background as 'intelligent working class'; Sir Edward Parkes, former chairman of the Committee of Vice Chancellors and Principals; Alan Smith, chief executive of the Test and County Cricket Board; and Bill Oddie, the comedian and actor. 'Our boast is that we are a classless school,' said Martin Rogers, the then chief master of King Edward's, where annual fees are about £4,000, roughly a third of Eton's. 'The leaders of Britain are now going to come from all over the country. The fact that you come from a certain school or university no longer means that you are destined for the top. We have the satisfactory position where people rise because of how they do their jobs.'

The *FT* index of top schools was dominated by former direct-grant grammar schools of the sort that threw in their lot with the independent sector in the 1970s. In second place was Manchester Grammar

School, whose alumni include Sir William Barlow, former chairman of BICC, the cables and construction group; Lord Sieff, honorary president of Marks & Spencer; and Howard Davies, director-general of the Confederation of British Industry. Other leading public figures to emerge from this 'new wave' of top private schools include Martin Sorrell, chief executive of the advertising group WPP, who left Haberdashers' Aske's with 10 O-levels and six A-levels, and went on to study at Cambridge; Sir Duncan Nichol, former chief executive of the NHS Management Executive, who is a former pupil of Bradford Grammar School; and Stanley Metcalfe, former chairman of Rank Hovis McDougall, and Chris Tideman, chief executive of the Burton group's retail services, who both attended Leeds Grammar School, which came tenth in the *FT* index of boys' public schools.

THE TOP INDEPENDENT SCHOOLS

Boys
1. King Edward's, Birmingham
2. Manchester Grammar School
3. St Paul's School
4. Winchester College
5. Eton College
6. Westminster School
7. The Haberdashers' Aske's
8. Bradford Grammar School
9. Royal Grammar School, Newcastle
10. Leeds Grammar School

Girls
1. St Paul's Girls' School
2. South Hampstead High School
3. North London Collegiate
4. Oxford High School
5. Wycombe Abbey
6. Withington High School
7. James Allen's Girls' School
8. The Haberdashers' Aske's School for Girls
9. Cheltenham Ladies' College
10. King Edward VI High School for Girls

Source: *Financial Times* survey of heads, examiners and admissions tutors, November 1990.

The wind of change, bringing with it a new élite, is blowing hardest through Britain's boardrooms. It will not be long before the pattern is repeated in all walks of life. In industry and commerce, international competition and economic stringencies have combined to force successful companies to reward achievement and embrace a more meritocratic culture. State schools have never had more representatives among the chairmen of the country's biggest companies. In 1990 Britain provided 20 of the top 30 corporate performers in Europe, and yet only one of their chairmen – Sir Anthony Tennant, an Etonian who was then chairman of Guinness – had attended a top-notch public school; seven of the chairmen went to grammar schools. Three years later, research at the London School of Economics was even more dramatic. It showed that 25 of the chairmen of Britain's top 50 companies – with a combined worldwide turnover equivalent to half the nation's gross national product – were educated in the state system; in 1989 there had been only 14. A further six attended former direct-grant grammars; only 15 went to public school, compared with 29 in 1979 – including nine to Eton, Charterhouse, Rugby, Shrewsbury or Winchester.

Announcing the results, Leslie Hannah, professor of business history at the LSE, emphasised the historic importance of his findings. 'The changes in the business élite seen in the past decade are more substantial than those recorded over all previous decades of the 20th century put together. All the signs are that the British business world is now substantially more meritocratic than it was a generation ago,' he said. 'The distinction between gentlemen and players is becoming as extinct at the top of British business as it has become in cricket.' Hannah insisted the change signalled the end of Britain's 'anti-industrial culture' and highlighted how the success of fee-paying pupils had fallen 'to the level one would expect in a meritocratic society'.

It is instructive to note which schools and universities members of the new élite attended, and it is even more crucial for parents to know where their potential successors are now being educated. Although any list is inevitably selective, here are 15 representatives – many of them honoured during the Thatcher years and most of them in their 50s or 60s – who have been standard-bearers for the new élite in British business:

Sir Peter Walters, 63, former chairman of Midland Bank: King Edward's School, Birmingham; Birmingham University.

Sir Allen Sheppard, 61, chairman of Grand Metropolitan PLC: Ilford County High School, Essex; London School of Economics.

Sir Eric Pountain, 60, chairman of Tarmac PLC: Queen Mary Grammar School, Walsall.

Sir Derek Birkin, 64, chairman of RTZ Corporation PLC: Hemsworth Grammar School.

Sir Denys Henderson, 61, chairman of Imperial Chemical Industries PLC: Aberdeen Grammar School; Aberdeen University.

Sir Michael Angus, 64, chairman of Whitbread PLC: Marling School, Stroud; Bristol University.

Lord Sterling, 59, chairman of P&O: Reigate Grammar School.

Sir Philip Harris, 51, chairman of Harris Ventures Ltd: Streatham Grammar School.

Lord Tombs, 70, former chairman of Rolls-Royce: Elmore Green School, Walsall; Birmingham College of Technology.

Alan Sugar, 47, chairman of Amstrad plc: Brooke House School, London.

Sir Richard Greenbury, 57, chairman and chief executive of Marks & Spencer: Ealing County Grammar School.

Sir Trevor Holdsworth, 67, chairman of National Power: Hanson Grammar School, Bradford, and Keighley Grammar School.

Maurice Saatchi, 47, chairman of Saatchi & Saatchi Co. plc: Tollington Grammar School; London School of Economics.

John Jennings, 57, chairman of Shell Transport and Trading plc: Oldbury Grammar School; Birmingham University.

Robert Evans, 67, chairman of British Gas: Old Swan College, Liverpool; Blackburn College; City of Liverpool Technical College.

Sir Ernest Harrison, 68, chairman of Racal Electronics plc and Vodafone Group plc: Trinity Grammar School, Wood Green, London.

Younger businesswomen, too, are at the forefront of the assault on the Oxbridge old-boy network. The challenge being mounted by an up-and-coming, thirtysomething generation of entrepreneurs, often from grammar schools and redbrick universities, is confirmed in an analysis of the background of 13,000 directors in more than 2,000 publicly quoted companies. The task, however, remains enormous, the result of generation after generation of the old order having it all their own way: a total of 535 directors, more than one in 25 of all those studied, attended an élite group of just 10 public schools; and 865, one in 15, went to Oxbridge; more than 300 had knighthoods. The number of women stood at a record 477, still only one woman for every 26 men but an increase of 12% in two years. Their average age was 46, compared with 53 for men; while nearly four in 10 women are under 40, the proportion for men was one in 10. Leslie Hannah says: 'It is international competition that has forced it [business] to be more professional, and to reward the competent and penalise the bad. The increase in the number of women is partly the result of political change, but it is also part of the same process. Businesses are waking up to the fact that there are a lot of able women out there, regardless of background.'

The shift against the old school tie approach is more noticeable in business and commerce than in the City, the civil service or many of the professions. Nicola Egerton-King, who at 32 is one of Britain's youngest directors, is typical of the new state-school generation. A former pupil of West Kirby Grammar School for Girls, with an economics degree from Bristol University, Egerton-King is finance director of SelectTV, makers of BBC series such as *Birds of a Feather* and *Lovejoy*. She is convinced she would never have reached such a senior level if she had gone into banking or manufacturing: 'The media is different because it is a fairly new industry.' Karen Jones, 38, managing director of the Pelican restaurant group, which owns the Café Rouge chain, claims that a 'young women's network' is emerging to counter the clubbiness of male-dominated boardrooms. Jones, who attended Mill Mount Grammar School for Girls in York before the University of East Anglia, said she was fortunate to have made her career in catering. 'It would probably have been different in other industries, but catering is very much a business where enterprising people work their way up. When I do come across other women at the same level in other industries, there is a real bond which can also be useful.'

TOP PRIVATE SCHOOLS FOR COMPANY DIRECTORS

1. Eton
2. Rugby
3. Marlborough
4. Winchester
5. Charterhouse
6. Harrow
7. Shrewsbury
8. Oundle
9. Uppingham
10.= Stowe
10.= Wellington

Source: Hemmington Scott Publishing, 1993.

TOP STATE SCHOOLS FOR COMPANY DIRECTORS

1. Aberdeen Grammar School
2. Bishop Vesey's Grammar School, Sutton Coldfield
3. Lancaster Royal Grammar School
4. Ayr Academy
5. King Edward VI School, Birmingham
6. Watford Grammar School
7. Bacup & Rawtenstall Grammar School, near Bolton
8. Dr Challoner's Grammar School, Amersham
9. Harrogate Grammar School
10.= Harrow County Grammar School
10.= King Edward VII, Sheffield

Source: Hemmington Scott Publishing, 1993.

TOP UNIVERSITIES FOR COMPANY DIRECTORS

1. Cambridge 448
2. Oxford 417
3. London 152
4. Manchester 109
5. Edinburgh 77
6. Leeds 65
7. Birmingham 63
8. Bristol 62
9. Glasgow 48
10. Sheffield 44

Source: Hemmington Scott Publishing, 1993.

For parents, it is necessary to second-guess the future. Even before the 'comprehensive-school generation' that left in the 1970s and 1980s – only one in 12 secondary pupils attended comprehensives in the mid-1960s – has risen towards the top of the pile, another revolution is under way. While the upper-class traditions of independent education have been diluted by an influx of 'first-time buyers', government reforms are producing a new and more readily identifiable hierarchy of state schools. The increasing diversity within the new class system is being reflected by more complex choices in education. As we have seen, rising numbers of able children with no family history of private education are attending fee-paying schools or a 'pick 'n' mix' combination of private and state schools; all but 150 or so grammar schools in a score of education authorities have disappeared; an élite of comprehensives is emerging out of a mass of egalitarian mediocrity; and a new breed of schools is being created with the introduction of 'semi-independent' grant-maintained state schools, the pioneers of which aspire to a similar status to that once held by direct-grant grammar schools. It may yet turn out that the comprehensive experiment was a temporary aberration that fails to yield more than a handful of members of the new élite; indeed, its alumni have so far barely penetrated the leadership of even the Labour party.

It is a lot easier these days to identify the most academically successful schools. Publication of examination results and the compilation of national league tables, for both the state system and the independent sector, give a scientific base to the sort of information that many aspiring and well-off parents have swapped over the dinner table or on the social grapevine. They have also highlighted how the best state schools are closing the gap on fee-paying rivals by achieving some of the highest A-level pass rates in the country. In the 1993 list of the top 250 schools at A-level there were places for a total of 49 state secondaries – five more than in the previous year, and including nine comprehensives. For the first time, a state school made it into the top 25, while four achieved a place in the top 50, compared with only one in 1992. The highest-ranking state school was Colchester County High School, a girls' grammar in Essex, where more than two in three A-level entries were awarded top grades and where expenditure per pupil was less than £2,300 a year. The Colchester grammar out-performed Cheltenham Ladies' College, where fees were £6,155 a year for day pupils, as well as Charterhouse (fees £7,110), Harrow (£12,360 for boarders) and Roedean (£11,985 for boarders).

An analysis of the types of schools listed in the top 250 highlights important trends: nearly half (116) were girls-only schools; more than a quarter (64) were boys' schools; and half the state schools (24) were grant maintained. More than half (127) were in London and the southeast of England, including 29 of the top state schools; only 79 of the 122 local authority areas in England, Wales and Northern Ireland were represented, while more than a quarter (77) of the schools were concentrated in only eight shire counties. Surrey had the biggest contingent with 11 schools in the top 250 – all of them private – followed by Kent, Oxfordshire and Avon (10 each).

THE TOP SCHOOLS FOR A-LEVELS IN 1993

State	Private
Colchester County High	St Paul's Boys'
Tiffin Girls', Kingston upon Thames	North London Collegiate
The Latymer School, Edmonton	Winchester College
Hasmonean High, Barnet	Manchester Grammar
Limavady Grammar, Limavady	King Edward's, Birmingham
King Edward VI Camp Hill, Birmingham	Westminster School
St Olave's, Orpington	St Paul's Girls'
Chelmsford County High	King Edward VI High, Birmingham
Tiffin Boys', Kingston upon Thames	Withington Girls, Manchester
Kendrick Girls', Reading	Bradford Grammar

THE TOP SCHOOLS AT GCSE IN 1993

State	Private
Beaconsfield High	St Paul's Girls'
Chelmsford High	Withington Girls, Manchester
Colchester County High	Lady Eleanor Holles, London
Ermysted's Grammar, Skipton	Queen's School, Cheshire
King Edward VI Camp Hill, Birmingham	Winchester College
King Edward VI Grammar, Stratford-upon-Avon	King Edward VI Girls', Birmingham
Lady Verney High, High Wycombe	Haberdashers' Aske's Girls
Queen Mary's High, Walsall	Guildford Girls' High
Newport High	North London Collegiate
Skipton High	Wycombe Abbey School
Wolverhampton High	King Edward's, Birmingham

Education is no longer clear-cut; just going to a public school does not necessarily put you ahead. There are good state schools and bad private schools. Which school you go to is less and less about the social cachet of its clientele and more about the quality of the education it provides. Even fee-paying schools are becoming more meritocratic. However, the chances are that you are more likely to find top-quality education in the independent sector where classes are routinely half the size of those in the state schools, with a pupil-teacher ratio of less than 11 to one. The new class warriors are not dogmatic: they are pragmatic consumers who pick the best of both worlds when it suits them. Their open-minded approach is particularly sensible in a period of flux and far-reaching change, the effects of which are far from certain. School and university are crucial stages of class development, and ones that weigh heavily in the balance when measuring your current class position. If the educational establishment, however, embraces the government's free market reforms of the state system, the public-versus-private dichotomy could evaporate even further. And the old class boundaries will blur even more.

CHAPTER FIVE

*F*OR RICHER OR POORER

MONEY is the root of all class. It is the solvent that dissolves old class distinctions and the oil that lubricates the new order; it is the great social liberator – the 'coined liberty' of Dostoevsky's memorable phrase. Wealth, however, is only a tool that can facilitate class ascendancy, not one that guarantees you have the edge on others. In the 1980s the amount you earned was almost as important as how you earned it. Today, the possession of wealth does not necessarily confer status, though it does enable you to exercise a greater freedom of choice: the docker who wins £2 million on the football pools does not immediately soar to the top of the class ladder, although the chances are he will move up much more rapidly than if he had not won a fortune.

The three-dimensional view of class recognises the importance of having a substantial income and the even greater importance of a 'disposable' income, the money left over after you have paid all the routine bills. Most of all, it takes account of how you spend your disposable income. Without money, it will always be a struggle to acquire any of the trophies that will lift you in the pecking order – a big house, a new car, private education and exotic foreign holidays. Poverty is a prison that strictly limits opportunities to improve your class position. If, however, it were simply a question of ranking people according to their financial standing, the art of class-spotting would be much easier. Although a well-paid job is obviously an advantage, it does not, in itself, automatically put you on a higher rung. Whether you are earning £20,000, £30,000 or £40,000 a year does not tell you where you are in the social order. Similarly, two people on exactly the same salary, or even with the same disposable income, could be worlds apart: one could have only recently won promotion from a humble job, while the other could have a long history of stable prosperity. How they use or express their wealth, both now and in the future, is often as important as how much money they have at their disposal. Somerset Maugham knew its proper significance: 'Money is like a sixth sense without which you cannot make a complete use of the other five.'

The poor are always with us. The misleading concept of 'relative poverty' makes that a certainty: you may be better off than you were, but if the rest are even better off then you are, the experts would have us believe you are actually worse off. Inevitably, the static and one-dimensional view of society that is most commonly adopted highlights the gap between the poorest and the wealthiest, which is quickly transformed, confusingly, into 'the poor' and 'the wealthy'; it also talks about the bottom 10% or 20% of households as if they always comprised the same people, trapped forever at the bottom of the pile in unremitting hardship. Also, more than one in 20, however, has in excess of £12,000 in savings, sometimes as a result of redundancy payments or other windfalls, evidence perhaps that their lowly position is only transitory; about a third are pensioners, whose average income has increased overall by more than a third in a decade.

The orthodox view of class reinforces and helps conserve the old order by concentrating on the relative distribution of wealth rather than the real improvement, in absolute terms, in the material prosperity of most individuals. Between 1978 and 1992, household expenditure increased by 66% in real terms; men's earnings went up by 30% and women's earnings went up by 50%; the overall income of the average person went up by more than a quarter; in 15 years the number of households on more than £600 a week, at 1993 prices, increased ninefold, from 230,000 to 1.2 million. In truth, more and more people are crossing the financial thresholds beyond which they can exercise serious class-determining choices: they have the wherewithal to buy houses, cars, holidays, shares and household luxuries that distinguish them from the rest of the crowd. A married man who is the sole wage-earner now has to work an average of only five minutes to pay for a loaf of bread, compared with nine minutes in 1971; or 35 minutes for 1lb of rump steak, compared with 56 minutes. Having less money than others does put you at a disadvantage, but it does not mean that you have to remain just another anonymous member of some soul-destroying 'socio-economic grouping'. It does not rule you out of the game, or interpose an insurmountable obstacle to class improvement.

The amount of personal wealth in Britain has increased phenomenally. In 1992 it stood at £2.3 trillion – that's £2,300,000,000,000, or nearly £40,000 for every man, woman and child; in real terms, it has increased by nearly three-quarters (72%) since 1978. A third of wealth is in the bricks and mortar of homes; about another third is 'non-marketable' because it is in life assurance or pension funds. In less than 15 years the amount of marketable wealth has shown a sevenfold increase, in cash terms, to £1,694 billion. It is usual to emphasise how unequal the distribution of wealth has remained, and how inequality has even been strengthened by the creation of an 'underclass'. The richest 1% own nearly one-fifth of marketable wealth, the same proportion as in 1976; and when the current social classifications were drawn up in 1913, the richest 1% owned 69% of the nation's wealth. However, the inequality in riches among a substantial proportion of the population is not as wide as many people might think, particularly if you include 'non-marketable' pension rights. Although nearly one in three is worth less than £5,000 and about one in six (16%) is worth £100,000 or more, the real battleground is in the middle: just over one in two people (52%) has net marketable wealth somewhere in the range of £5,000 to £50,000. Nearly one in four adults (24%) is worth between £25,000 and £50,000. Among these, more than anybody else, it is impossible to classify individuals on wealth alone.

While it requires time and opportunity to amass a fortune by owning your own business, getting a well-paid job often provides a fast track up the class ladder. Indeed, with more than 2 million unemployed, one of the deepest social divides now is between those in work and those out of work. Of course, it is even better if you are in one of the three-in-10 households that have two earners; in contrast, one in three (32%) households has no wage-earners at all.

We read so often about the six-figure salaries of business executives and media celebrities that it is easy to have an exaggerated view of what people really earn. As a result, it is assumed that there is a huge gulf between the earnings of the old middle class and the rest. It is worth knowing that, at most, one in five employees earns more than £20,000 a year – and that is before tax. After the Inland Revenue has done its worst, the proportion drops to about one in eight. Four in 10 – a total approaching 10 million people – take home between £10,000 and £20,000; nearly six in 10 take home between £7,500 and £20,000. Just as with wealth, it is in the crowded middle ground of earnings that the class war is at its most intense and where other factors decide whether you are keeping up with the Joneses, or even edging ahead.

DISTRIBUTION OF TOTAL INCOME

	Before Tax Number and % of taxpayers	After Tax Number and % of taxpayers
£3,445–£4,999	2.2m (9%)	2.7m (11%)
£5,000–£7,499	3.9m (16%)	4.8m (20%)
£7,500–£9,999	4.0m (16%)	4.5m (18%)
£10,000–£14,999	6.1m (24%)	6.2m (25%)
£15,000–£19,999	3.9m (16%)	3.5m (14%)
£20,000–£29,999	3.2m (13%)	2.1m (9%)
£30,000–£39,999	1.0m (4%)	0.5m (2%)
£40,000 or more	0.8m (3%)	0.3m (2%)

Source: Inland Revenue Statistics 1993.

The three-dimensional view of class reveals how the shape of society is no longer the pyramid suggested by current social classifications. At the same time that the middle is becoming more crowded, the distance between the highest earners and the lowest earners is growing. The linear hierarchy is getting longer and, like a tall, slightly top-heavy man with an expanding waistband, more and more egg-shaped. Two-fifths of income is earned by one-fifth of the population: the top 20% has increased its share of income to 40%, while that of the bottom 20% has fallen to 5%. One in 10 employees earns less than £153 a week, while one in 10 earns more than £510.

The orthodox view of class is that 'white-collar' office workers are higher up the class hierarchy than 'blue-collar' workers on the shop-floor. In 1971 the official social classification system highlighted the distinction by splitting Social Class III into manual and non-manual subsets: Class III (M) and Class III (N). Both are of equal status, notionally at least, although market researchers are more honest in ranking them as C1s and C2s. To rank one occupational grouping higher than the other, however, can no longer be sustained, certainly not simply on earnings. The cloth-capped miner scraping a living in his two-up, two-down terraced house, spending every evening in the pub and every weekend racing pigeons is not just a stereotype – it is a parody of a working class that no longer exists. It is perpetuated by members of the old middle class desperate to maintain a condescending sense of superiority and 'separateness' by clinging on to a comforting black-and-white snapshot of social divisions. In today's social spectrum, class divisions are so blurred at the edges that they run into each other; the picture is not so much black and white, as different shades of grey. On average, a coalface miner earns about £25,000 a year and can, in a productive year, earn as much as twice that. As likely as not, he will live in a modern, four-bedroom detached house in a North Yorkshire market town, have a taste for good wine and play a round of golf before socialising with friends in the local clubhouse.

It is true that, overall, the gap between earnings in non-manual and manual occupations has grown gradually over the past five years or more: the average manual worker earns £13,300 a year, or £5.92 an hour for a 43-hour week, while the average non-manual worker has a salary of £18,200 or £9.08 an hour for a 38-hour week. However, there is a great deal of overlap: nearly one in four manual workers actually earns more than the average non-manual worker. And more than one in four non-manual workers still earns less than the average manual worker. At its most extreme, one in 10 manual workers earns more than £391 a week, while the same proportion of non-manual workers earns less than £153. The old-fashioned distinction that asserts the superiority of the 'white-collar' worker and the inferiority of the 'blue-collar' worker is a distortion of the truth.

Increasingly, it is recognised that your age, or rather your 'lifestage', can exert an enormous influence over your class position. Whether you are married or living with a partner, whether – and when – you have children, the size and age of your mortgage, whether you have ageing relatives living with you, all these can affect your financial position. In the United States there is a saying that when you are 30 you should be earning $1,000 a year for every year of your life; by the time you are 40, you have not really made it unless you are bringing home $2,000 a year for every year of your life. The successful career-minded thirtysomething couple who suddenly find themselves reduced to a single income and a huge mortgage when they have children in quick succession can find themselves slipping down the social pecking order, while a middle-aged couple who have had routine manual jobs for most of their lives can hit their peak after their children have left home and as their mortgage is paid off just as they reach their maximum earning potential. The average household income in 1992 was £343 a week. However, the proportion of households headed by somebody in their 40s and with an income of more than £800 a week was one in eight, compared with one in 16 overall. Conversely, only one in 30 of the same fortysomething households had an income of £60 or less, compared with one in 18 overall. Whatever your career or employment history, there is a time of life when you are in your prime when it is relatively easy to scale the class ladder.

There is a special place for the élite of the super-rich, so rich they cannot count it. They really are in a league of their own. Beyond a certain threshold, money is important for itself, not the extra possessions or lifestyle it can buy. In terms of social cachet, there is a limit to the number of houses and cars any one person can own. Who are the super-rich? And are they always the same people, each from a similar mould? The most definitive answers come from the *Sunday Times* lists of Britain's rich, compiled by Philip Beresford since 1989. In successive years, these lists have provided the most authoritative guide to up to 500 of the wealthiest of Britain's estimated 20,000 millionaires and handful of billionaires. Even though the individuals who figure in the lists are, inevitably, extraordinary people, the changing composition of the wealthiest of the super-wealthy is a touchstone by which to test the extent of social change and to discover some clues to the kind of people who are shooting up the social ladder. Close analysis shows two things: firstly, the remarkable stability of 'old money' in the hands of a tiny number of aristocratic families; secondly, the extent to which a new élite, with a cast that varies from year to year, can amass huge fortunes, often from scratch in a single lifetime. The former is an unsurprising hangover from the fag-end of a feudal past; the latter is a signpost to a more dynamic future. Ironically, it is the new élite that has often helped the rich aristocrats to stay rich, by buying their land and property, by creating a lucrative market for their art treasures and by building successful companies for them to invest in.

In the 1993 *Sunday Times* list of Britain's 400 richest, with assets worth a total of £55 billion (more than three-quarters of Britain's social security budget) there were 12 dukes, seven marquesses, seven viscounts, 20 earls and 19 lords – a total of 65 aristocrats, plus the Queen. They included the owners of the top 10 art collections in private hands; in addition there were 33 knights. There were 59 Etonians, 11 Harrovians and 64 who went to Oxbridge. However, while 182 had inherited fortunes, the majority could best be described as self-made. Indeed, 87 were not worth even £1 million when Margaret Thatcher became prime minister. It is instructive to consider where and how most of the fortunes were made: 72 in commerce and retailing; 56 in industry; 44 in property and construction; 36 in food and drink; 28 in music, sport, entertainment and films; 20 in media; 18 in banking and finance; and 63 were millionaires after selling their companies.

In the top 200 alone, there were more than 30 people – worth a total of £4 billion – who did not inherit their fortunes, started from remarkably ordinary beginnings, frequently attended state schools or, in a minority of cases, lesser public schools, and made their money by responding to the spirit of the age. They can truly be regarded as the richest standard-bearers for the new élite. Only two of the 'stock market superstars' of the 1980s – Alan Sugar, of Amstrad, and Michael Green, of Carlton, – remained sufficiently prosperous to figure in all five lists published since 1989. Others have fallen from the highest point of the roller-coaster of new money because of the recession and the slump in shares or property prices. The 'quickly come, quickly go' careers of many multi-millionaires is evidence of the vibrancy of an enterprise culture that has the old order under siege. It shows that behind the apparently unchallenged supremacy of the landed aristocracy there is a swirl of social change; after all, the members of the new élite who fall out of the list of the 400 richest can hardly be counted as poor as a result. The relative transience of new money is a symptom of how fluid the class system has become. In 1867 Walter Bagehot wrote: 'The order of nobility is of great use . . . not only in what it creates, but in what it prevents. It prevents the rule of wealth – the religion of gold.' More than a century later, it is failing in its historic task and beating a stiff-upper-lipped retreat: wealth based on achievement is finally getting the upper hand on a dwindling nobility based on an accident of birth. It is true that some members of the new élite sometimes become quasi-aristocrats by being made lords and ladies, a process aimed at heading off the challenge to the old class hierarchy by absorbing the would-be challengers; the Vesteys, the billionaire butchers, bought their title from Lloyd George in 1922 for £20,000. More often, however, others eschew such baubles of public recognition. About half of the richest 400 do not even have a mention in *Who's Who*: their wealth speaks for itself. In the list below there are 20 people who clearly epitomise the achievements of the new élite, often emerging from 'ordinary' family or educational backgrounds to score meritocratic success by their own efforts and with an entrepreneurial flair that embodies the spirit of the age:

Richard Branson (£475m, 16th), 43, chairman of Virgin empire: Stowe School.

Paul McCartney (£400m, 19th), 51, musician: Liverpool Institute.

Jack Walker (£320m, 21st=), 63, former steel tycoon and owner of Blackburn Rovers: left school at 14; not in *Who's Who*.

David Thompson (£300m, 23rd=), 58, chairman of Union Square plc: Haileybury; ISC; former Smithfield meat-trader.

Elliott Bernerd (£130m, 69th=), 49, chairman of Chelsfield plc; left school at 16 to become estate agent.

Elton John (£120m, 76th=), 47, musician: Pinner County Grammar School; Royal Academy of Music.

Alan Lewis (£100m, 89th=), 56, textile tycoon who started work at 15 in a printing firm; not in *Who's Who*.

John Madejski (£100m, 89th=), 52, former newspaper sales executive who founded *Auto Trader*; not in *Who's Who*.

Anita (and Gordon) Roddick (£100m, 89th=), 41, founder and managing director of Body Shop: Worthing High School for Girls; Bath College of Education.

Cameron Mackintosh (£90m, 103rd=), 47, musical producer: Prior Park College, Bath.

Sir Philip Harris (£85m, 109th=), 51, chairman of Harris Ventures: Streatham Grammar School.

Paul Sykes (£85m, 109th=), 51, son of a Barnsley miner who became first businessman to earn £6m a year in 1989; not in *Who's Who*.

Peter Kindersley (£80m, 113th=), 52, chairman of Dorling Kindersley: King Edward VI School, Norwich.

Ann Gloag (and Brian Souter) (£80m, 113th=), 51, managing director of Stagecoach Holdings: Perth High School.

Alan Sugar (£65m, 143rd=), 47, chairman of Amstrad plc: Brooke House School, London.

John Apthorp (£60m, 148th=), 59, chairman of Wizard Wine: Aldenham School.

Mark Knopfler (£60m, 148th=), 44, member of Dire Straits pop group; former local journalist; not in *Who's Who*.

Peter Waterman (£60m, 148th=), 47, former British Rail fireman turned disc jockey and record producer; not in *Who's Who*.

Michael (and David) Green (£50m, 182nd=), 46, chairman of Carlton Communications plc: Haberdashers' Aske's School.

Sir John Hall (£50m, 182nd=), 61, chairman of Cameron Hall Developments Ltd: Bedlington Grammar School.

Wages and salaries are not the only source of income; in fact, they now make up less than two-thirds of all household income, compared with three-quarters 30 years ago. Other sources on the increase are investments, pensions, self-employment and, for the less well-off, social security benefits. To have a personal portfolio of shares used to be a distinguishing mark of the old middle class. However, since Margaret Thatcher's push towards a share-owning democracy, that is no longer the case. The big privatisations of the 1980s mean that stocks and shares now have mass appeal. There are nearly 10 million shareholders – more than one in five (22%) of the adult population and more than three times the number when Thatcher came to power; most of them still own shares only as a result of privatisation issues, although 200,000 'first-time buyers' went on to buy a stake in non-privatised companies. The southeast of England has 39% of all shareholders, followed by the southwest, 10%; West Midlands and northwest, 9%; Scotland, 8%; Yorkshire and Humberside, 7%; East Midlands, 6%; the North, East Anglia and Wales, 4%.

Most significantly, about one in seven (15%) shareholders are people in the lowest two social classes; surprisingly, only one in three shareholders is from the top two classes and more than half (52%) are C1s and C2s. So ownership of shares remains a useful class discriminator, but not one that in itself distinguishes as powerfully as in the past between a relatively small, wealthy élite and the rest of the population. It has penetrated much further down society. Today, it is a question of what sort of shares you own, how many, and what their value is, particularly since the proportion of UK-quoted equities owned by personal shareholders has fallen sharply – from two-thirds in 1957 to just over one-fifth in 1992. Almost half of all shareholders (49%) hold shares in more than one company, up from 40% in 1990. Nearly one in five (18%) has shares in only two; nearly one in 10 (9%) has shares in three companies. One in six (17%) has shares in four to 10 companies, a 50% increase in three years, while one in 25 (4%) has shares in 11 or more. By this measure, then, you really need to have shares in at least four companies if you want to be regarded as a serious player.

WHO OWNS SHARES?

Occupational group	% Shareholders	% Owners of privatised shares	% Owners of non-privatised shares
AB	33	36	36
C1	29	28	29
C2	23	23	21
DE	15	13	14

Source: NOP/Treasury survey of share ownership, 1993.

Among shareholders there are five clearly defined categories. The pecking order is:

Traditional shareholders: They own non-privatised shares; they may also own privatised shares, but will have bought them after other shareholdings (18% of shareholders, about 1.6 million people).

New share-owners: They first bought privatised shares as an introduction to shareholding before going on to buy shares in non-privatised quoted companies (2% of shareholders, about 200,000 people).

Sids: They own privatised shares only, including TSB; they own no shares in non-privatised companies except perhaps as employees or relatives of employees (62% of shareholders, about 5.7 million people).

Employee-only shareholders: They own shares as a result of employment or the employment of a relative; they hold no other shares (10% of shareholders, about 960,000 people).

Abbey National shareholders: They own shares but only in Abbey National, which gave £100-worth of free shares to all customers (8% of shareholders, about 800,000 people).

Owning shares is a sign that you have staked your claim to a place in society. It says that you are not simply a wage-slave, but someone who is prepared to look beyond the day-to-day and risk hard-earned cash to invest in the future. It is estimated there are about 5.7 million people who have bought shares themselves and still hold them. Far and away the biggest group comprises the 'Sids', who account for nearly three in four (74%) share-buyers. They have swollen the ranks of the new middle class and sounded the death knell of the 'them-and-us' society.

One of the most powerful indicators of your financial standing is the amount of debt you can run up. Your credit rating is a cornerstone of your class rating. The amount of personal credit given by banks, building societies and finance houses more than doubled during the 1980s; since 1976 it has trebled in real terms, excluding borrowing for house purchases. Cash and property are no longer the only currency of class. The total amount of 'plastic money' spent in 1993 was close to £50 billion; more than three-fifths of that went on credit cards, with the rest on debit cards. Every second of every day nearly £1,000 is spent by credit card, which is now the most popular way of buying goods costing more than £50. In 1992, there were 721 million credit-card transactions, with more than 1,200 transactions every minute – each worth an average of £43 – ringing up a turnover of more than £80m every day, a figure that has shown a sixfold increase in 10 years. In 1992 alone, there was a 9% fall in the number of cheques written compared with the previous 12 months.

CREDIT COMMITMENTS

	% adults
Mortgage	37
Credit card	32
Charge card	25
Mail order	21
Retail store account	15
Bank loan	6
Bank overdraft	6
HP/Credit sale	5
Finance house loan	4

Source: *Financial Research Survey, GB, October 1992–March 1993*, NOP Corporate and Financial, 1993.

No self-respecting working-class family used to contemplate getting into debt, certainly not for the routine luxuries of life. Neither a lender nor a borrower be was the refrain: you can't spend what you haven't got. Today you buy now and earn later. Your Visa card or Mastercard is the entry ticket to the full-blown consumer society: 10p in every pound spent by consumers is with a credit card. Within 30 years since their launch, Britain has accumulated a pile of 27 million cards, half of them in the past decade, in the hands of about one in two adults, even if they do not all use them. About one in three cardholders are occupational As and Bs, but the same proportion are C1s and about a quarter are C2s. Even the Ds and Es make up about one in eight cardholders. The credit boom has liberated the less well-off and given them the chance to cash in on the confidence they have about their own upward mobility. It means that ordinary people can walk into Harrods or any other 'top people's store' and make the sort of impulse buys that were once the luxury only of the rich.

But do not believe that everyone who wants a credit card has one, even in a country that is the heaviest user of credit cards in Europe: half of all applications are rejected. Most commonly they are single people, those under 29, lone parents, the unemployed and low-income households. Simply having a credit card says a lot about you, just as having a bank account – held by four in five adults – was once a prize cherished for its social exclusivity. Having a bank account is now a truly classless trait. What matters more is where you keep your cash, and whether it is with Coutts & Co, Clydesdale or the Co-op. Banks can have distinctly different types of clientele: Lloyds customers, for instance, spend the most on personal financial services; NatWest is the small-businessperson's bank; Abbey National, the building-society-turned-bank that offered shares to all its account holders, is the high street upstart for the new middle class; and the Co-op makes a play for clean-living, environment-friendly socialists.

WHO HAS CREDIT CARDS?

Occupational class	% Cardholders
AB	32
C1	33
C2	23
DE	13

Source: *Financial Research Survey, GB, October 1990–March 1991*, NOP Corporate and Financial, 1991

Excluding mortgages, about one-fifth of all consumer borrowing is made on credit cards. A total of £9 billion was outstanding at the end of 1992, with the average for each cardholder being less than £420; half of all credit-card bills are cleared every month; and two in three cardholders have outstanding debts equivalent to less than one-tenth of their credit limit; only one in 25 is within 10% of the limit. In short, the richer you are the more you borrow.

There are some cards that say more about you than cash ever can. An élite within the community of credit cardholders uses plastic to assert its superiority rather than to ease its cashflow. Such are the gold cardholders: more than one in 50 credit cards is 'gold', only occasionally available to those whose earnings are less than £40,000 a year. (The minimum for a Coutts gold card is £75,000.) Gold cards generally have no-questions-asked limits of £10,000, compared with the average of £1,400 on an ordinary credit card. Aimed at jet-setting executives, they also come with a bundle of perks that include cheap loans, free travel insurance, emergency cash and card replacement, and free legal helplines. Annual fees for such privileges can be as much as £120. Who are the fortunate few who have turned debt into a sought-after symbol of success?

Detailed studies of the lesser-spotted gold cardholder have been conducted by American Express, still a market leader, even though its image has been occasionally tarnished by top restaurateurs refusing to accept it. Their findings reveal not only the personal wealth of hundreds of thousands of high-achievers, but also their lifestyles and leisure activities. Amex gold cardholders, of which there are an estimated 200,000, have an average income of £41,000 a year (about twice the national norm). They would not even consider themselves wealthy unless they earned at least £100,000 a year, and a substantial minority would not regard themselves as rich until their annual income topped £500,000.

The results provide an insight into the preferences of the new middle classes; one in five Amex gold cardholders has a second home, often on the Continent; nearly a quarter invest in art and antiques; six in 10 endure 'working breakfasts'; half own stocks and shares; a third have cleaners. The typical user takes three holidays a year, often travelling long hauls to the Caribbean or the Far East; three-quarters have recently drunk champagne; one in five had a mobile phone as early as 1990, well ahead of the herd; the same proportion has three cars, one of which is almost certain to be a BMW; and four in five keep fine wine at home. So there you have it: the success story of the upwardly mobile consumer.

There comes a point, however, when socially acceptable credit descends into the embarrassment of debt. More than 2 million households have to contend with debts they are unable to service. Their plight is the other side of the coin: in the eyes of others, they seemed secure in their elevated class position. In fact, they were living beyond their means and suddenly their world came crashing down. The 1980s bestowed financial freedoms but it also laid new traps. The credit boom made it possible for millions to climb the class ladder, even if many were subsequently to slide back again. It vastly increased the amount of social mobility, both up and down. Its legacy has heightened our awareness of the importance of wealth in the same way that Oscar Wilde came to understand it: 'When I was young I thought that money was the most important thing in life; now that I am old, I know it is.'

Inheritance has always been one of the easiest routes to wealth. 'Saving is a very fine thing,' Sir Winston Churchill said, 'especially when your parents have done it for you.' It used to be only the rich who inherited the Earth; now it is a fact that most people will have a chance of coming into a sizeable cash windfall at some time in their lives. The wealth of previous generations is increasingly visited upon sons and daughters from very ordinary backgrounds; about one in eight households (12%) has benefited from some sort of inheritance. The amount of money and property passed on may not equal that of the family heirlooms, landed estates and Old Masters of the aristocracy, but it does help improve or reinforce the class potential of millions of people; it can also help stop the slide of the downwardly mobile by allowing them to live off the money of wealthier parents. For a small minority, a surge in inheritances will mean the revival of long-forgotten rentier-class lifestyles such as those portrayed in P.G. Wodehouse comic novels; for many more, it will provide the escalator to a higher level.

THE TOP 10 WILLS OF 1992

	Estate net value
Earl Spencer	£88m
Harry Joel Joel, racehorse-trainer and breeder	£41m
Francis John Baring, Lord Northbrook	£31m
Comtesse Barbara de Brye, Australian property heiress	£30m
Sarah Gredley, widow of Bill Gredley, racehorse owner	£15m
Harold Ivan Leech, former brush salesman who inherited family fortune of long-lost cousin	£12m
Edward William Fattorini, former managing director of Grattan mail-order giant	£11m
Francis Bacon, artist	£11m
Anthony Samuel Edgar, former chairman of H. Samuel, jewellers	£11m
Sir Rowland Austin Smith, former chairman of Ford	£10m

Source: *The Sunday Times*, 1993.

Following his vision of a 'classless society', John Major said in 1991 that he wanted to see 'wealth cascade down the generations'. He insisted: 'We don't wish to see each generation starting anew, with the past cut off and the future ignored.' It is all right, it would seem, for social mobility to be inherited, too, even in a 'classless' society: you can build on the class foundations laid by your upwardly mobile parents and other relatives. A watershed for many, however, is whether or not they are children of parents who took part in the rapid expansion of home-ownership during the post-war period and particularly the Thatcher era, which enabled more than 1.5 million people to buy their council homes. The implications of the revolution in home-ownership, one of the biggest motors of social change in Britain in the second half of the 20th century, have still to be fully realised.

The 1990s' recession and the housing slump – property accounts for half the value of the average estate left when somebody dies – have caused only a momentary setback to an inheritance bonanza that has already soared to £14 billion a year. Home-ownership rates, only about 56% in 1981, are expected to continue to rise to a peak of 75% by the year 2005, inevitably resulting in more heirs suddenly becoming better off. Within 20 years there will be 21 million home-owners, including nearly nine in 10 (86%) pensioners. Consequently, by the turn of the century, the number of property inheritances, which numbered only 88,000 in 1981, should have risen to 200,000 annually; by the year 2011 they will have almost doubled from current levels to 235,000. Their value will approach £35 billion a year and, as a result, members of more than one in 50 households will inherit property worth an average of £75,000. Even now, the proportion is over one in 100 households inheriting property worth an average of £30,000 – and that is even before the full impact of changing patterns in owner-occupation has hit home: Inland Revenue figures show the number of 'houses passing on death' remained at between 70,000 to 110,000 throughout the 1980s, with about half of all people still dying with assets of less than £5,000. As the inheritance bonanza grows and spreads, it will create a further layering of the social order, with those who inherit little or nothing falling behind their contemporaries in the second great home-owning generation.

Inevitably, inheritance still has the biggest effect on the old middle class, whose members – usually in their mid-40s to 50s – can expect to benefit from the cumulative effect of wealth cascading down several generations; for them, heritable wealth holds out the promise of big cash windfalls and an untroubled, prosperous retirement. While the moderately well-off have been caught in the 'inheritance trap' and had to sell inherited property at the bottom of the housing market, the less well-off – many of whose parents were the first home-owners in their family – are becoming eligible for small fortunes. Within the past three years the proportion of estates valued between £100,0000 and £140,000 has halved to less than 4%, while the proportion valued from £40,000 to £70,000 has risen to 25%; just under half are valued at less than £40,000.

WHO LEAVES THE WEALTH?

	% of inheritances
Parents	59
Grandparents	13
Uncles and aunts	18
Brothers and sisters	3
Other relatives	4
Non-relatives	3

Source: NOP survey of 10,644 households, 1992.

How much you are likely to inherit depends not only on whether your parents were home-owners, but also on where they lived. Because it is a function of the property market and has the same regional and cyclical differences, wide discrepancies exist between the wealthiest and poorest counties in terms of average inheritances. The wealthiest counties in England and Wales are: Oxfordshire, £107,433; Surrey, £99,124; West Sussex, £93,239; Wiltshire, £89,574; and Buckinghamshire, £88,869. The poorest are: Mid-Glamorgan, £43,491; West Glamorgan, £51,410; Durham, £51,899; Cleveland, £53,066; and Lancashire, £54,066. In 1992 London escaped the reversal in fortunes caused by the recession and the property slump, according to figures compiled from more than 240,000 wills registered at Somerset House. In the capital the value of the average will increased by 14% to more than £108,000, compared with £59,954 in Wales and £60,220 in the northwest of England. Of course, for the super-wealthy it is almost irrelevant where you live: in 1992 the number of millionaire legacies – one in every 500 estates – increased to 537, while nearly one in 100 estates – a total of 2,171 – was valued at £500,000 or more.

HOW WE SPEND INHERITANCES

	%
Investments	46
Consumption	14
Buy business	2
Pay mortgage	36
Buy property	18
Home improvement	13

Source: NOP survey of 10,644 households, 1992

The proceeds of inheritance serve a dual purpose. They provide financial security; indeed, even the prospect of coming into a substantial chunk of money and property, however far off it might be, adds to the confidence of would-be heirs. The proceeds also provide a swift increase in material prosperity, not least because the beneficiaries most frequently are in, or approaching, a relatively comfortable middle age with reduced overheads and small mortgages. Nearly four-fifths of inherited property is sold, most of it being put on the market immediately. In the long term, half of all heritable wealth is spent on consumption, even though initially it may be invested or used to reduce mortgages. Inheritance on a mass scale, rather than within a small self-perpetuating élite, enhances opportunities for social mobility and acts as a catalyst for class improvement. But in an ageing population the scale of change may be constrained by the elderly spending their legacies before they die, whether on Saga-style holidays or nursing home fees. Anyway, the successful class warrior should not simply wait for such a windfall. The early acquisition of wealth is the surest foundation of upward mobility.

CHAPTER SIX

CLASS OCCUPATIONS

*I*T is ironic that it was an aristocrat who epitomised one of the fundamental cultural shifts of the past decade. Six years after Margaret Thatcher came to power, Alexander Patrick Greysteil Hore-Ruthven, poet, academic, economist and the 2nd Earl of Gowrie, decided his £33,000-a-year salary as Minister for the Arts was simply not enough to sustain a London lifestyle. The Earldom of Gowrie, an ancient Scottish title revived in the last century, brought with it neither a landed estate nor a stately home; even an aristocrat, owner of a Covent Garden flat and a modest family home in Herefordshire, was unwilling to afford the luxury of a career in public service. 'I am a self-employed businessman,' pronounced Gowrie, previously a partner in a successful firm of Mayfair art dealers, 'who has worked now for the Government and the State for six-and-a-half years, and inevitably that has been an extremely expensive interruption of my business career.' At the age of 45, Lord Gowrie – 'the sort of man who will never walk if he can hail a taxi' – said he had to think about earning some money for his old age. By 1994, after seven years as the £150,000-a-year European chairman of Sotheby's, with an estimated £1.5 million of share options, the Etonian's old age was sufficiently secure for him to venture forth again into the public arena as the unpaid, part-time chairman of the Arts Council.

The three-dimensional view of class goes beyond traditional social classifications, which have become ossified over time. The class hierarchy created by the occupational As, Bs, C1s, C2s, Ds and Es is now completely outdated, a throwback to a bygone era when 'public service' and the 'professions' were put on a pedestal. It has penalised millions of women who have been classified according to the occupations of their partners as 'heads of household', while earnings have been largely ignored so that a poorly paid parish priest ranks with a high-profile national television interviewer on a lucrative contract. Above all, traditional classifications have taken little account of how certain jobs and the people who hold them have moved up and down in public esteem. Even with a more holistic approach, a redefinition of the pecking order of occupations will be regularly required to reflect such movements. Overall, however, the likelihood is that the new élite will be found in the world not of public service, but of private enterprise.

To base a new system of social classification on a reordering of the old occupational hierarchy would be over-simplistic, ignoring the importance of people's backgrounds, cultural tastes and ambitions. Nevertheless, in the eyes of many, what you do for a living remains the embodiment of your class. 'The basic principle of English social life is that everyone (everyone, that is to say, who comes to the front door) thinks he is a gentleman,' wrote Evelyn Waugh. 'There is a second principle of almost equal importance: everyone draws the line of demarcation immediately below his own heels. The professions rule out the trades; the services, the professions; the Household Brigade, the line regiments . . . it is essentially a process of ruling out.' Within the three-dimensional view, your occupation is a cornerstone of class, as crucial in defining your social standing as your education, personal wealth and whether you own your own home. The question then becomes: what is the new pecking order of occupations?

The status of many traditional middle-class jobs has taken a battering over the past 20 years. In the days of the British Empire, public servants pursued respectable careers in Africa, India and other far-flung parts of the colonial establishment. Literally, they were the inventors of red tape. Today, however, they are more likely to be found in their native country, running their own little empires in central and local government. The furthest their horizons extend is to an all-day seminar in Brussels about the latest European Union directive on waste disposal. The mystery of an exotic posting has been replaced by the tedium of everyday minutiae: it is no surprise that these 'shop-floor bureaucrats' have suffered such an erosion of status that they now rank alongside even the most ordinary of clerical and office workers.

The professions, for generations an exclusive middle-class 'closed shop', have also suffered a decline. In almost every case the iniquity of the privileges they enjoy has been exposed, and their class position undermined. In law, barristers have been forced to share a stage with solicitors, many of whom now have the right to represent clients in the higher courts. Even solicitors are on the slide: for years, they cloaked the mysteries of much of their work in arcane language and elaborate secrecy. They were finally exposed in the housing boom of the 1980s when thousands of home-buyers became 'do-it-yourself' conveyancers and found that it was remarkably straightforward. Many firms, some of which earned up to 80% of their income from house sales, had to fall back on state hand-outs in the form of legal-aid work. Of course, the biggest beneficiaries among the new 'subsidariat' – the middle-class spongers of public funds – are farmers: instead of scratching a living from the land, barely a day goes by without them setting off in their Range Rovers to find out where the next Common Agricultural Policy grant is coming from. In a world where subsidies is a dirty word, their standing is not high. The scandal of 'set aside', the policy under which farmers get paid for growing nothing, has tainted the image of a sturdy, self-reliant breed who get up at all hours in all weathers to feed the nation.

As the 'subsidariat' grows, so does the size of the new professional proletariat. The teaching profession, as once it was, has led the way: ever since the classroom chaos and school strikes of the 1980s, teachers have surrendered any hope of reinstating themselves in public esteem in pursuit of better pay and working conditions. Their behaviour aped that of the 1984 miners' strike, and achieved almost as much. In the aftermath of the explosion of higher education and the transformation of polytechnics into 'new universities', academics are in danger of becoming two a penny; moreover, they have lost their biggest perk – the rights of tenure and a job for life.

The differentiation between the professions and the rest of the workforce is increasingly blurred; their importance is largely residual. Long gone are the days when members of the professions were the cream of the workers who relied simply on their mental abilities rather than their physical strength: by the year 2000, it is estimated that 70% of all jobs will require 'brains' rather than 'muscle', which was true of only 30% of jobs in 1945. The widespread introduction of performance-related pay – the white-collar equivalent of industrial productivity agreements – has also weakened the standing of the professions as something separate and superior. Teachers, town hall staff and even the police have been singled out for payment by results.

Many professions have been tainted by national scandals. Social workers have suffered badly as a result of a catalogue of child-abuse blunders, culminating in outrage over the removal of Orkney children from their families. The police have lost public respect over their handling of such cases as the Birmingham Six and the Guildford Four; the armed forces have been eaten away by successive cuts that have highlighted their diminished role in the new world order. Estate agents, who used to be at the heart of the professional classes, were derided in the late 1980s, replacing second-hand car dealers as the epitome of sharp practice. Gazumping, gazundering and fanciful descriptions of properties for sale made estate agents so notorious that they had to be regulated by new laws to keep them in line.

Architects and town planners, who enjoyed an inflated public reputation during the 'new town' era of post-war reconstruction, have taken a spectacular fall as urban utopias crumbled into inner-city nightmares. Prince Charles touched a nerve when he led the attack on the 'monstrous carbuncles' of contemporary architecture. The recession has taken a heavy toll on architects, many of whom are among the most downwardly mobile professionals with average earnings of about £23,000 a year and high levels of unemployment.

The downturn in the economy has claimed other victims. Accountants have lost kudos since the burden of their business moved towards insolvency practice, winding up failing companies and 'ambulance-chasing' the casualties of the recession. In the aftershock of the Big Bang in the City, self-styled financial consultants – in reality, little more than the 'man from the Pru' – quickly lost their gloss after gaining a reputation for hard-sell techniques more commonly associated with double-glazing salesmen. The turmoil at Lloyds, the British institution that is the apogee of the insurance world, sent tremors far and wide, impoverishing hundreds of wealthy and influential middle-class people and shaking public confidence in the City and many of those in it.

Bank managers, more than any other professionals, are in a spiral. At the peak of their social standing, they used to be – along with vicars – archetypal 'pillars of the community': confidants, counsellors and caring supporters acting in the best interests of customers. They were instrumental in ensuring that small businesses flourished locally. Such is their fall from grace that some bank managers are now reluctant even to confess their occupation. They have been attacked for putting the banks' interests ahead of those of account holders, for abdicating responsibility for their decisions by deferring to head office, and for adopting a short-term approach that has unnecessarily doomed viable businesses to failure because of temporary difficulties. The inevitable result has been a sharp decline in public esteem, compounded by garish television advertising – in which bank managers are noticeably absent – and inane slogans such as 'We're here to make life easier' (NatWest), 'The listening bank' (Midland), and 'The bank that likes to say yes' (TSB).

Politics has always been a part-time profession: the traditional timetable of parliament is geared to the gentlemanly routine of barristers, senior business executives and the rural gentry. Never has the electorate been so disillusioned with its politicians, caught up in a web of incompetence, scandal and sexual indiscretion. In fact, the composition of the House of Commons has never been less different from the rest of the population. After John Major's election success in 1992, Conservatives from state schools outnumbered those from private schools for the first time by 177 to 159. An analysis by Parliamentary Monitoring Services revealed a decline in Tories with a military or landed background, putting businessmen in the driving seat: one in three Tory MPs described themselves as company directors, slightly more than those that came from the professions. The 'new model' Labour party had 271 MPs, of whom 13 went to private school; the single most dominant occupational group comprised university, college and polytechnic lecturers (48, or 18%), closely followed by teachers (43, or 16%); another 46 (17%) were trade union officials or party workers.

Why is the current crop of parliamentarians such a collection of political pygmies? Is it, as the loyalist *Daily Telegraph* has implied in its leader columns, that such a 'sorry lot' are the result of the Tory party turning away candidates from traditional Conservative backgrounds such as Eton and the squirearchy? 'What has emerged, in place of the old knights of the shire, is,' the newspaper insisted, 'a host of frankly inadequate men and women who, far from entering Parliament in any spirit of public service, are driven solely by the pursuit of self-advancement.' In truth, the difficulty arises out of successfully attracting people from a broader range of backgrounds into an environment created over centuries to suit the needs of a tiny minority. Real talent is deterred by low rates of pay, poor working conditions and lack of power. Few MPs are members of the new élite, and hardly any of the Cabinet.

The new élite are agents of social change. They are neither a profession nor members of a club, and shun the traditional barriers to entry such as a public school accent or Oxbridge education. They do not simply respond to society, they help to shape it. The jobs they do reflect the active role they play, and are often to be found in 'lifestyle' or service industries such as media, travel and holidays, and retailing. They are the people who package off-the-shelf upward mobility and sell it to the masses: they are 'egalitarian capitalists' with a mission to make affordable once-exclusive possessions to ordinary consumers. Their hall of fame could include Henry Ford, the car maker, Sir Freddie Laker, the airline operator, and Sir Jack Cohen, the 'pile 'em high, sell it cheap' founder of Tesco. Frequently, they are also opinion-formers with the ability to have their voices heard. They are less likely to work in traditional manufacturing, heavy industry or the public sector; they are the 'doers' in a 'can-do' culture. Above all, they live in the present, are unencumbered by their past but are driven by an ambition to be the best.

The essence of the new élite is revealed in the *Sunday Times* list of Britain's 500 richest people. After five years at the top of the list, the Queen was replaced in 1994 by Gad and Hans Rausing, two Swedish-born brothers who own TetraPak, makers of milk and fruit-juice cartons. The pair, who left Sweden in the early 1980s to escape its high taxes and settled in Britain, are thought to be worth £5.2 billion, £200 million more than the Queen. The 1994 list also confirms that Britain is becoming more meritocratic: the split between self-made millionaires and inherited wealth used to be about 50/50, now 'old wealth' accounts for only 28% of those named. Although more than one in five (137) made their money from property and land, commerce and retailing (128) came a close second, while industry (95), food (50) and music (33) were also important sources of wealth.

In the new pecking order of occupations, jobs in the media, whether print or broadcast, are near the top. (Twenty-four of Britain's 500 richest made their money from the media, according

to the *Sunday Times* list.) Those who work in it are imbued with a
status and influence that is often out of all proportion to the
effectiveness or importance of the work they do. Simply being
there is enough; staying there, however, is sometimes difficult.
Only on television could a weather presenter become an icon,
and a newsreader be venerated as an authority. The media has
been transformed by technology and the ending of 'Spanish
practices' that dated back to the medieval guilds. Despite individual
examples of nepotism, the industry is remarkably open to all
comers: even the BBC has been forced to be less hidebound and
more meritocratic. Newspaper editors and media tycoons exert
influence so enormous that the careers of Cabinet ministers,
company chairmen and showbusiness celebrities can rise or fall at
their whim. Lower down the pecking order, even the most humble
television researcher or cub reporter can impress by taking advantage of the privileges of being 'in the media'.

It is in the boardroom that members of the new élite are most
noticeably supplanting the old guard. Their progress is particularly
prominent in sectors such as retailing, technology and the privatised
utilities: David Sainsbury, who recently took charge of the family
supermarket empire; Anita Roddick, founder of the Body Shop; Sir
Geoffrey Mulcahy, executive chairman of Kingfisher, which owns
B & Q, Woolworth, Comet and Superdrug; Ed Wallis, chief
executive of PowerGen, the electricity company; and Stafford
Taylor, former boss of the Cellnet mobile phone network, who is
in charge of BT's personal communications division.

One of the most fertile areas for breeding the new élite is that of
management buy-outs, which blossomed in the 1980s as entrepreneurial managers – and enthusiastic workforces – in seemingly less-
than-successful enterprises were given the chance to escape the
restraints imposed by unenterprising owners. Many companies that
thrived under the new regimes went on to even greater success when
they were floated on the stock market, making millions of pounds for
those involved. There has been a marked increase in the number and
value of management buy-outs: in 1980, 100 deals were worth £40
million; in 1992 the comparable figures were 520 buy-outs totalling
more than £3 billion. A year later, 33 companies formed by buy-
outs joined the rush to the stock market – three times more than in
the previous year and the highest number for five years.

One of the biggest management buy-outs was the National

Freight Consortium (NFC), hailed as a triumph for 'popular capitalism'. Thousands of lorry drivers, tea ladies, clerks and typists plundered their savings to buy out NFC from the government in the early 1980s. Such was the success of the transport company that by 1989 each £1 originally invested had come to be worth £74. The average holding of the 10,000 NFC workers who put up money at the outset was £44,000, while at least 400 employees were worth £250,000 when the firm's shares were quoted on the Stock Exchange for the first time. More recently, with contracting out of services, an increasingly common practice within both the public and private sectors, management consultants are the new freelance trouble-shooters who earn as much as £1,000 a day by selling their skills to put companies on the right track: Sir John Harvey-Jones, former chairman of ICI, has made a career out of it for himself and many like him.

Of all the social groups, the self-employed and other owners of small businesses are the most enduring examples of individualism. Since 1979, their numbers have risen sharply to 5 million; despite the recession, more than 400,000 people decided to be their own boss in 1993. Many of those opting for self-employment risked the money they received from redundancy settlements in nationalised industries and the declining manufacturing sector. They cover a wide range of occupations, from highly paid computer technicians to menial jobbing gardeners. They fit uneasily into traditional occupational groups, which use the size of the workforce to determine the social class of the self-employed, because their businesses often employ no more than 10 people. They are penalised by the very characteristic that makes them successful – the smallness of their business. Some are among the most upwardly mobile: even electricians and plumbers who work for themselves are distinguished by their wealth and lifestyles that set them apart from others in the same trade who are employed by big companies.

Celebrities from the world of entertainment, whether pop stars, composers or actors, have taken on an importance that extends beyond the stage on which they perform. Frequently enjoying international renown, their lifestyles are the subject of unprecedented scrutiny. Many have exploited the opportunities that fame brings to build business empires of their own: Sir Andrew Lloyd Webber, the 'unofficial royal composer' whose hits include *Cats*, *Phantom of the Opera* and *Sunset Boulevard*; Paul McCartney, one of

Britain's richest people and a substantial landowner; John Cleese, the former Monty Python star, who has become a successful producer of business training videos.

Those who pander to the new élite also become part of it, not merely as appendages but as their peers. The most successful are pioneers in their own right. Most obvious are the fashion designers, restaurateurs and assorted 'superchefs' who clothe and feed high-profile achievers. Prue Leith, a former businesswoman of the year and a bestselling writer, epitomises the phenomenon, as do Anton Mosimann, the world-class chef, Sir Terence Conran, the design guru, Bruce Oldfield, couturier to the rich and famous, and Paul Smith, one of the leaders in designer-label menswear.

Even in the unpromising milieux of the 'old professions', there are opportunities for some. In the universities, academics who become cultural entrepreneurs by popularising their subjects and knowledge have graduated to household names: Stephen Hawking, author of *A Brief History of Time*; Michael Wood, the television archaeologist; Malcolm Bradbury and David Lodge, the novelists; and Baroness Warnock, the philosopher and moralist. In the Church of England the historic decision to allow the ordination of women is certain to elevate the social standing of women within the church establishment, producing a female élite among the clergy. On the shop-floor there are signs that old hierarchies are tumbling: the 'them-and-us' divisions that reinforced the inferior status of manual employees are being replaced, particularly in Japanese-owned factories, by 'flat' management structures that allow workers and managers to share responsibility, to eat together in staff canteens and to mix socially out of working hours.

In the 1980s, there was a prevailing belief that there was no status like money. That may no longer be true: money, in itself, does not confer social standing. It does, however, provide the means by which aspiring individuals can pursue a better quality of life at the same time as possessing the trappings of success. The gap between the highest earners and the most impoverished welfare claimants has never been greater; the fundamental divide is between the employed and the unemployed. While the Continent has largely resisted change, 15 years of Tory rule have helped to make Britain's once-rigid workforce more flexible. Trade union privileges and workers' rights have been eroded, minimum wages scrapped and jobless benefits cut. Productivity has risen by an average of nearly 5% a year since 1979 – the fastest rate of any major industrialised country. But the changes have had a big social impact: they have left Britain with a low-paid, low-skilled workforce, and levels of unemployment that show little sign of abating. With one-sixth of the European Community's population, the United Kingdom accounts for one-quarter of its poor; 10 million people earn less than the Council of Europe's 'decency threshold'.

Inevitably, the size of your salary is a key to determining whether you can afford a lifestyle that can attract as much social standing as the nature of your occupation once offered. A well-paid factory worker can 'buy' higher status than an impoverished office clerk. Similarly, there is little point in having one of today's most esteemed occupations if you are paid a pittance. Why be a low-paid television researcher surrounded by glamorously wealthy opinion-formers if it means you have no chance of ever earning as much as a moderately successful civil servant or town planner? Equally, there is nothing to be gained by sticking in an 'old profession' unless you can count on rising to the top. The most prosperous members do, after all, still enjoy impressive benefits of success: they live in big houses, send their children to public school and drive luxury foreign cars. Consequently, there is a balance to be struck between being poor in a high-status job and wealthy in a staid occupation. As ever, those with the greatest aspirations seek the best of both worlds.

PAY POWER

Occupation	Typical annual earnings
Commercial QC	£750,000
Senior director of big company	£500,000
Top footballer	£500,000
Leading hospital consultant in private practice	£300,000
Criminal QC	£200,000
Creative director in advertising	£175,000
National newspaper editor	£160,000
Partner in firm of solicitors	£100,000
NHS consultant	£90,000
Police commissioner	£90,000
High Court judge	£87,500
Professional jockey	£85,000
Public school headmaster	£60,000
Top clinical psychologist	£55,000
Account director in advertising	£50,000
GP	£40,000
Head of state secondary school	£40,000
National newspaper journalist	£40,000
Top osteopath	£40,000
Police chief superintendent	£38,000
BBC TV producer	£35,000
Oxford University professor	£35,000
Air traffic controller	£33,250
Homeopath	£30,000
Oil-tanker driver	£25,000
London Underground driver	£23,000
British Rail train driver	£20,000
Schoolteacher	£20,000
London taxi driver	£19,500
Legal secretary	£18,000
Police constable	£17,000
Motorcycle courier	£15,500
Lorry driver	£15,000
Nurse	£15,000
Provincial newspaper journalist	£15,000
Driving test examiner	£14,500
Social worker	£14,500
Bus driver	£13,000
County cricketer	£12,000
NHS porter or caterer	£6,500

CHAPTER SEVEN

A HOME OF YOUR OWN

ONCE it was the way you spoke, who you voted for and what you did with your spare time that were used by others to judge your social class. Today, you are more likely to be judged by where you live. From inner-city nightmare to country dream cottage, the roof above your head is a key class indicator. Possession is the overriding factor: homeownership, enjoyed or endured by more than two-thirds of the population, is a peculiarly British obsession. A casual conversation with a stranger may begin with what you do for a living, but it will invariably move on quickly to your home and the size of your mortgage. Unlike traditional social classifications based on occupational groups, the three-dimensional view of class takes full account of the significance of owning your own home. The paradox, of course, is that most 'homeowners' do not actually own their homes in the conventional sense. They are mortgaged to the hilt and the mortgage lender, usually a bank or building society, has an entry on the title deeds until the day the debt is settled. In an objective sense, the quality of life of many owner-occupiers is no better than that of those who rent. Indeed, burdened with huge borrowings and therefore having less disposable income, home-owners may actually be worse off. Yet, in the social pecking order, they have achieved a higher status because they are perceived to be worth at least the value of their homes, and are confident that their long-term employment prospects are promising enough to meet the monthly repayments on a 20- or 25-year mortgage.

Since the days of the Norman Conquest, power and status have been expressed through ownership of property. However, the view that your home not only provides a roof over your head but is also a sound investment is a fundamental tenet of the middle class. It was in the 17th century, following the Restoration of the monarchy, that the rights of property were made sacrosanct so that for the first time an ordinary Englishman's home became as impregnable as an aristocrat's castle. From that moment a buoyant trade in buying and selling homes developed as owners took advantage of the new stability in property. Thus was created the estate agents' profession. So deeply held is the view today that your home is a good investment that many owner-occupiers have refused to accept the fall in property prices in recent years; thousands of families have chosen to stay put and denied themselves the chance to move to a better area rather than lower the selling price of their existing property to find a buyer in a depressed market.

Where you live is probably the grandest and most influential of all public statements about your social standing. It is a reliable indicator because virtually all householders express their individuality through the bricks and mortar they inhabit. Ownership of your home remains a crucial definer, saying much about your confidence in the future: the mortgage is the ultimate symbol of this confidence, as it is only those in secure jobs with good career prospects who can seriously contemplate taking one out. What is striking is that for decades only the middle class had the confidence to take on such a lifetime of debt; today, members of the old working class are equally bold.

The property boom of the 1980s brought with it a class revolution. It churned the social order and made a nonsense of the traditional occupational hierarchy. For example, car workers in Oxford who paid next to nothing for only modest homes 25 years ago suddenly found they were sitting on a fortune, and were able to cash in their assets and retire early to the coast or live a life of leisure abroad. Others used the capital as security to set up in business, climbing the social ladder among a new breed of entrepreneurs.

Some were not so fortunate. Even those in well-paid jobs were struggling if they were too late in staking a claim in the property market. As prices rocketed, they found the best they could afford was a two-bedroomed terraced house in a street where neighbours with much lower earnings had already paid off their tiny mortgages. Worse was to come: when the slump came at the beginning of the 1990s, they were trapped in homes worth less than they had paid for them. They became the downwardly mobile of the housing market, victims of 'negative equity', whose attempts to improve themselves are in limbo while they wait for property values to increase once more.

Despite such setbacks, we remain infatuated with homeownership. Lured by Margaret Thatcher's housing reforms and generous tax breaks on mortgages, the British are converts to the middle-class philosophy that you can never say you have made it until you have a place to call your own. It is distinctively middle class because you can earn the right to a Surrey mansion, but it takes an accident of birth to entitle you to the landed estates of the upper class. The suburban idyll, with its leafy avenues and immaculate lawns, is what most of us aspire to. But with increased crime and traffic congestion disturbing even the tranquillity of Acacia Avenue, some people are seeking something more: peace of mind. And that can be found in some unfamiliar corners of the British Isles.

Statistics confirm the rise of the most basic of middle-class values. Homeownership has leapt over the past 20 years: in 1971 less than half the households in Britain (49%) were owner-occupied compared with 54% by 1981 and 67% by the beginning of the 1990s. Council tenants have been seduced by the vision of the 'property-owning democracy', particularly when they were offered inducements to buy their homes for less than £1,000. Thatcher's right-to-buy legislation of 1979 enabled more than 1 million local authority tenants to cross the threshold of the property market. The spread of homeownership has meant that in terms of one-upmanship, it is the minutiae that counts – the number of bedrooms, age of construction, size of garden and so on. Owner-occupiers are easy to spot on council estates across the country. One of the first things they do is replace their corporation-green front doors with mock-Georgian or cottage-style porches. Next is the satellite dish, fixed in full public view like a coat of arms proclaiming their new-found independence from rentbook neighbours.

So important is the ownership of your own home that the one in three householders who rent privately or from a local authority are certain to languish near the bottom of the social scale. There is a world of difference, however, between council tenants, who receive accommodation by virtue of need or a willingness to wait on a list, and the vicars, public school teachers and officers in the armed forces whose homes come with the job. But such perks are no substitute for title deeds. One quarter of all homes are owned outright without the encumbrance of a mortgage, a consequence of the post-war baby-boom generation that was the first to aspire to homeownership *en masse*.

THE PROPERTY-OWNING DEMOCRACY

	% of households
Owner-occupied, with mortgage	42
Owner-occupied, owned outright	25
Rented from local authority or New Town	21
Rented privately	7
Rented from housing association or co-operative	4
Rented with job or business	2

Source: *General Household Survey*, 1992.

Owning your own home is the launchpad for the aspiring class warrior. The big question then becomes how much it is worth. Everyone has a maximum beyond which they cannot afford to go, and a minimum below which they would not countenance sinking: one man's ceiling is another man's floor. A house 'blessed with character' is what most of us are after and are willing to pay a premium to get. Modern is definitely out, and volume house-builders such as Charles Church, Barratt and Bovis have pandered to the new nostalgia by constructing 'period' homes embellished with eaves and gables that evoke an age of individual craftsmanship and H.E. Bates's *The Darling Buds of May*. The popularity of such properties is rooted in a desire to be part of a long home-owning tradition; a modern house suggests that you are a latecomer to the ranks of homeowners proud of a more established prosperity.

What is the pecking order of the property market? The most sought-after homes are those built before the end of the Second World War. In general, inter-war properties, most of which can be found in the suburbs, are the most valuable after brand new ones, which are expensive largely because of the high cost of construction. An inter-war detached house or semi is actually a better investment than a new one. Victorian and Edwardian semis are relatively rare and worth more than similar properties from other eras.

HOME VALUES

	Pre-1919	1919–45	1946–60	Post 1960 (not new)	New	All
	£	£	£	£	£	£
Terraced	48,530	49,320	43,550	48,280	53,000	48,640
Semi-detached	79,650	60,220	52,770	51,950	53,480	58,490
Detached	126,390	126,580	118,890	92,780	95,950	102,610
Bungalow	56,740	74,070	74,340	65,920	65,390	67,920
Flat/maisonette	54,620	45,460	41,220	42,110	48,310	47,920
All	60,920	64,760	60,220	61,200	71,650	62,770

Source: Halifax Building Society, 1993.

Whatever the value, the type of property you live in is one of the most defining statements of class. Aside from the beautiful terraces of Westminster, Bath and Edinburgh, terraced houses will always be synonymous with the working-class poor of cities spawned by the industrial revolution. The 'detached' property has just that purpose in mind: to detach you from the riff-raff by means of the grounds that surround it. It is the prerequisite of all but the most cosmopolitan well-off. But it is semi-detached suburbia, synonymous with the middle classes, that has triumphed over other property types. The Metroland vision of Sir John Betjeman, with its 'leafy lanes in Pinner', has spread throughout Britain. This once-maligned British phenomenon has seen off its critics, who attacked its uniform design, manicured gardens and the petty-mindedness of its owners. Today the semi-detached way of life is celebrated by writers who have come to appreciate how it has successfully combined the seemingly contradictory virtues of privacy and neighbourliness.

But not every middle-class member aspires to the sort of suburban havens conjured by the house names of Dunrovin and Rosedene. In recent years the gentrification of traditional working-class areas has blurred class boundaries. From Islington in north London to Jericho in Oxford, from Albert Dock in Liverpool to Headingley in Leeds, virtually every British town has seen its former artisan districts become fashionable among young, well-educated high-flyers. They are the high priests of the 'cult of the individual'. They have rejected the anonymity of suburbia that has burgeoned with the expansion of the middle class. Unable to afford the country houses of the upper classes, they have moved down-market in an attempt to stand out from the crowd. Even Sloane Rangers, the traditional middle class, have gentrified parts of southwest London that were once the homes of those in their service. The tribal settlements of the gentrifiers can easily be identified: their neighbourhoods are clogged with cars and they defend to the death their extended territory of residents-only parking spaces; at dockside developments, entrances are guarded by security staff, while high walls and gates keep out unwanted visitors; the nearest corner shop sells ripe Brie and freshly squeezed orange juice, but rarely gives shelf space to processed cheddar, potted meat and cans of Tizer.

WHERE WE LIVE NOW

	% of households
Semi-detached	30
Terraced	28
Flat/maisonette	18
Detached	15
Bungalow	9

Source: General Household Survey, 1993.

It is, however, the extent of your territory that can really put you ahead. Fewer than one in 30 have a second home in the United Kingdom, whether it is a house, a flat, a caravan or a houseboat. Even fewer own property abroad. The size of your property can also set you apart: only 12% of households have seven or more rooms, excluding the bathroom and lavatory. And, of course, nothing reveals your social status quite like the size of your garden; more than one in 10 households do not even have one.

HOME TERRITORY

	% of households
2 rooms (or one)	2
3 rooms	8
4 rooms	21
5 rooms	33
6 rooms	23
7 or more rooms	12

Source: General Household Survey, 1990.

Every lifestyle accessory adds to the list of social signifiers: furnishings are particularly important. Being upper class is not having to buy your own furniture; their homes are filled with priceless heirlooms, while those of the traditional middle class are also distinguished by collections of antiques, fine porcelain and silverware, although usually on a more modest scale. The new élite, however, are more at ease with modern objects: in the early 1980s, the 'G-Plan Generation' favoured white-emulsioned walls and splashed out on high-tech fitted kitchens, black leather furniture and designer spotlights. Now they have succumbed to the 'new nostalgia' of the 1990s, opting for flowered wallpaper, antique Oriental carpets and reproduction Welsh dressers. Mass production has cheapened the high-tech look and sent them in search of a habitat that is more idiosyncratic and that creates an atmosphere of individual craftsmanship.

Of all home décor, net curtains are the most revealing. There are 'nets' with intricate paisley-style patterns, others that cascade down windows in ruffles. Almost all of them are of dubious taste. The upper classes seldom resort to them, because they are so rarely overlooked on estates miles from the rest of civilisation; the same is true for those of the middle class who inhabit detached houses in large grounds. For the old working class and even many members of the middle class they provide a comforting shield against the prying eyes of passers-by in semi-detached suburbia or city terraces. Gardens, however, are the best way to put some distance between you and your neighbours. They can also reinforce your position in society: a mature garden, even if it is measured only in feet, is imbued with well-established prosperity, while planting fast-growing conifers is evidence only that you are *nouveau riche.*

It used to matter whether you lived north or south of a line running between the Severn and the Wash. Above the line – 'somewhere north of Watford' – you were the poor relations of those beneath it. Depressed house prices in the north reflected 'inferior' status, aggravated by industrial decline. By the mid-1980s, southerners, the main beneficiaries of the property boom, could look forward to trading in a three-bedroom semi for a luxury mansion in the north, should they ever wish to live there. But this was not always the case. The Wessex novels of Thomas Hardy tell us that the south, too, was once impoverished, and not that long ago. In the 19th century standards of living were generally higher in the industrial towns of the north than many rural parts of southern England. George Orwell, writing in the 1930s, reinforced the view: 'It is a fact that poverty – extreme poverty – is less in evidence in the industrial north than it is in London. Everything is poorer and shabbier, there are fewer motor-cars and fewer well-dressed people; but also there are fewer people who are obviously destitute.'

The latest recession, which hit the most prosperous areas of the country hardest, has eroded the north-south divide: Margot of Surbiton can no longer look down her nose at Mavis of Sheffield. Britain is emerging from the downturn a more homogeneous society, in which few of the traditional distinctions between north and south remain. In the early 1990s, house prices fell most sharply in Greater London, the southeast and East Anglia. But in the north of England, Wales and Northern Ireland, prices actually rose during the recession. Regional differences in the number of homeowners have also narrowed. In the decade to 1991, the proportion of owner-occupiers rose from 48% to 61% in the north; in Greater London it rose from 52% to 62%. The conclusion is clear: you no longer have to live in the Home Counties to be middle class.

Although the north-south divide may be fading, it has not disappeared altogether. A decade ago, houses in the southeast, then the most expensive part of the country, cost 75% more on average than Yorkshire and Humberside, the cheapest region. Today, properties in the most expensive area – Greater London – cost 50% more than the north of England, now the cheapest region

in mainland Britain. Northern Ireland still lags a long way behind
the rest of the United Kingdom.

HOW MUCH YOUR HOUSE IS WORTH

Area	1983	1993	% increase
Yorks & Humberside	£23,090	£52,436	127
Northwest	£25,580	£56,133	119
West Midlands	£28,220	£61,680	119
East Midlands	£26,140	£54,483	108
North	£25,230	£51,738	105
Wales	£25,880	£52,366	102
Scotland	£28,930	£57,091	97
East Anglia	£30,090	£58,827	96
Greater London	£39,820	£76,408	92
Southeast	£40,590	£76,219	88
Southwest	£33,060	£61,448	86
Northern Ireland	£25,720	£39,756	55
United Kingdom	£30,900	£62,564	102

Source: Halifax Building Society, 1993 (fourth quarter).

It is not enough simply to own a mansion with swimming pools,
squash courts and stables. If the house is in the centre of Birkenhead,
Castleford or Walsall, then any social status that others might
bestow on you is severely undermined. Neighbourhood is all-
important. When British Telecom introduced its telephone code
changes for London in 1991, hundreds of people living in the outer
suburbs demanded to be issued with 071 numbers primarily
designated for inner London. They complained that the 081 code
for outer London they were to receive would depress the value of
their homes. It was unacceptable to let everyone know you lived
away from the West End, Kensington and the City.

Such geographical snobbery is particularly prevalent in Scotland
and Wales, often referred to dismissively by the English middle class
as the 'Celtic fringe'. The residents of Edinburgh, proud of staging
Britain's biggest cultural festival each year, have long believed they
are superior to Glaswegians; in turn, the Glaswegians point out that
culture comes to Edinburgh for one month a year and is conspicu-
ously absent the rest of the time. Cardiff citizens, too, regard their

city, with its grand government buildings, as superior to Swansea. In fact, they are probably right.

When it comes to the right address, few of these places fit the bill. Unwittingly, the Council Tax, which replaced the Community Charge in 1992, has provided a new and authoritative social barometer to compare the status of residential areas. Every property in Britain has been valued and placed in one of eight groups: Band A, the lowest, is for homes worth less than £40,000 in England (below £30,000 in Wales, and £27,000 in Scotland) while band H, the highest, is for homes valued at more than £320,000 in England (above £240,000 in Wales, and £212,000 in Scotland). Some householders have already recognised the social significance of this and sought to have their tax band raised, rather than lowered, to maintain the sheen of affluence.

The Council Tax data provides a unique guide to Britain's well-heeled areas and has thrown up some intriguing disparities. It shows that it is not just the working class who congregate in 'ghettoes', and identifies those areas of the country where the middle class are most prevalent. What it reveals is that parts of Surrey, Hertfordshire and London remain the best places to live if you want to make an impression: Kensington and Chelsea, with nearly one in five properties worth more than £320,000, ranks as Britain's most exclusive neighbourhood; Elmbridge in Surrey is probably the most upmarket all-rounder with virtually no homes worth less than £40,000 and one in 20 valued at more than £320,000.

The list of top districts – 49 in all – with more than one in 100 properties in band H also identifies many prosperous enclaves dotted around the country: Macclesfield and its environs, in the heart of the Cheshire stockbroker belt, are among an élite few outside the southeast, with one in every 50 homes worth more than £320,000; Stratford-upon-Avon and the Cotswolds follow closely behind, while the Ribble Valley in Lancashire, a traditionally affluent farming area, is also near the top. In Scotland, two areas stand out: Bearsden and Eastwood, both in Strathclyde. The omissions from the list are instructive: apart from Sevenoaks, there appears to be nowhere in Kent that is particularly upmarket, while Bedfordshire is the only county in the southeast not to be represented.

THE COUNCIL TAX BAROMETER

Local authorities with the biggest proportion of homes in band H	%
Kensington and Chelsea, Inner London	17.8
Westminster, Inner London	12.8
South Buckinghamshire	5.9
Elmbridge, Surrey	5.1
Chiltern, Buckinghamshire	4.7
Camden, Inner London	4.6
Three Rivers, Hertfordshire	4.0
Tandridge, Surrey	3.9
Waverley, Surrey	3.9
Richmond upon Thames	3.3
Barnet, Outer London	2.9
Guildford, Surrey	2.9
Hammersmith, Inner London	2.9
Mole Valley, Surrey	2.7
Bearsden, Scotland (Strathclyde)	2.5
Sevenoaks, Kent	2.6
Chichester, West Sussex	2.4
Runnymede, Surrey	2.4
Eastwood, Scotland (Strathclyde)	2.3
City of London	2.2
Windsor and Maidenhead, Berkshire	2.1
Epping Forest, Essex	2.0
Macclesfield, Cheshire	2.0
Stratford-upon-Avon, Warwickshire	2.0
Cotswolds, Gloucestershire	1.9
Hertsmere, Hertfordshire	1.9
Merton, Outer London	1.8
Reigate and Banstead, Surrey	1.7
Winchester, Hampshire	1.7
East Hampshire	1.6
Kingston upon Thames	1.6
St Albans, Hertfordshire	1.6
Tweeddale, Scotland (Borders)	1.6
Woking, Surrey	1.6
Uttlesford, Essex	1.6
Horsham, West Sussex	1.5
Edinburgh	1.4
Wandsworth, Inner London	1.4
Wealden, East Sussex	1.4
Brentwood, Essex	1.3
Harrow, Outer London	1.3

The Council Tax Barometer—contd

Oxford	1.3
Ribble Valley, Lancashire	1.3
Salisbury, Wiltshire	1.3
South Oxfordshire	1.3
Surrey Heath	1.3
Kincardine, Scotland (Grampian)	1.2
Newbury, Berkshire	1.2
Test Valley, Hampshire	1.2
Vale of Glamorgan, Wales	1.2
East Hertfordshire	1.1
East Lothian, Scotland (Lothian)	1.1
Hounslow, Outer London	1.1
Kennet, Wiltshire	1.1
Warwick	1.1
Welwyn Hatfield, Hertfordshire	1.1

Local authorities with the smallest proportion of homes in band A

	%
City of London	0.0
Bearsden, Scotland (Strathclyde)	0.1
Harrow, Outer London	0.1
Islington, Inner London	0.1
Kingston upon Thames	0.1
Camden, Inner London	0.2
Elmbridge, Surrey	0.2
Epsom and Ewell, Surrey	0.2
Richmond upon Thames	0.2
Sutton, Outer London	0.2
Croydon, Outer London	0.3
Woking, Surrey	0.3
Bromley, Outer London	0.5
Eastwood, Scotland (Strathclyde)	0.5
Kensington and Chelsea, Inner London	0.5
Broxbourne, Hertfordshire	0.6
Hillingdon, Outer London	0.7
Barnet, Outer London	0.8
Watford	0.8
East Hertfordshire	0.9
Welwyn Hatfield, Hertfordshire	0.9

Source: Department of the Environment, Welsh Office and Scottish Office.

BRITAIN'S MOST AFFLUENT AREAS

The local authorities common to both tables.
Barnet, Outer London
Bearsden, Scotland (Strathclyde)
Camden, Inner London
City of London
East Hertfordshire
Eastwood, Scotland (Strathclyde)
Elmbridge, Surrey
Harrow, Outer London
Kensington and Chelsea, Inner London
Kingston upon Thames
Richmond upon Thames
Welwyn Hatfield, Hertfordshire
Woking, Surrey

The conclusions are obvious and the advice simple: avoid the northeast of England. Humberside, County Durham and Tyne and Wear are littered with towns and cities that are pure working class. By contrast, the West Midlands, West Yorkshire and the northwest emerge, surprisingly, unscathed. None is prominently featured in the council tax data as over-burdened with cheap homes or bereft of upmarket properties. Only Barnsley and the city of Manchester stand out as working-class ghettoes. The data reveals that even the southeast has its blackspots: Hertfordshire, which is rated as one of the most exclusive counties in Britain, also accommodates Stevenage, which comes near the bottom of the pile. Hackney, in London, features as a place to avoid except, perhaps, for exponents of inverted snobbery. Wales has a dearth of valuable properties, although neither it nor Scotland possesses many homes worth less than £30,000. Strathclyde has some of the best and worst neighbourhoods in Britain.

WORKING-CLASS GHETTOES

Local authorities where at least two in three properties are in band A	%
Easington, Durham	85
Wansbeck, Northumberland	76
Derwentside, Durham	75
Kingston-upon-Hull	74
Scunthorpe, Humberside	74
Sedgefield, Durham	73
Manchester	71
Cumnock, Scotland (Strathclyde)	70
Sunderland, Tyne and Wear	70
Wear Valley, Durham	69
Liverpool	68
Nottingham	68
South Tyneside, Tyne and Wear	68
Barnsley, South Yorkshire	67
Bolsover, Derbyshire	67
Burnley, Lancashire	67
Gateshead, Tyne and Wear	67
Great Grimsby, Humberside	67

Local authorities with barely any homes in band H
Aberconwy, Wales
Adur, West Sussex
Alyn and Deeside, Wales
Arfon, Wales
Ashfield, Nottinghamshire
Barking and Dagenham, Outer London
Barnsley, South Yorkshire
Barrow-in-Furness, Cumbria
Bexley, Outer London
Blaby, Leicestershire
Blaenau Gwent, Wales
Blyth Valley, Northumberland
Boston, Lincolnshire
Broxtowe, Nottinghamshire
Cannock Chase, Staffordshire
Carmarthen, Wales
Ceredigion, Wales
Chesterfield, Derbyshire
Chester-le-Street, Durham

Working-class ghettoes—contd
Clydebank, Scotland (Strathclyde)
Colwyn, Wales
Copeland, Cumbria
Crawley, West Sussex
Cynon Valley, Wales
Delyn, Wales
Derby
Dinefwr, Wales
Dwyfor, Wales
Easington, Durham
Fenland, Cambridgeshire
Gateshead, Tyne and Wear
Gillingham, Kent
Gloucester
Glyndwr, Wales
Great Grimsby, Humberside
Hackney, Inner London
Harlow, Essex
Hartlepool, Cleveland
Hereford
Ipswich, Suffolk
Islwyn, Wales
Kingston-upon-Hull
Kingswood, Avon
Knowsley, Merseyside
Langbaugh-on-Tees, Cleveland
Llanelli, Wales
Lliw Valley
Luton, Bedfordshire
Manchester
Mansfield, Nottinghamshire
Meirionnydd, Wales
Merthyr Tydfil, Wales
Monklands, Scotland (Strathclyde)
Montgomeryshire, Wales
Motherwell, Scotland (Strathclyde)
Neath, Wales
Newham, Outer London
Newport, Wales
Northampton
North Tyneside, Tyne and Wear
Nuneaton and Bedworth, Warwickshire
Ogwr, Wales
Orkney
Penwith, Cornwall
Plymouth

Working-class ghettoes—contd
Port Talbot, Wales
Preseli Pembrokeshire, Wales
Radnorshire, Wales
Rhondda, Wales
Rotherham, South Yorkshire
Rhuddlan, Wales
Rhymney Valley, Wales
St Helens, Merseyside
Sandwell, West Midlands
Scunthorpe, Humberside
Shetland
Slough, Berkshire
Southampton
South Ribble, Lancashire
Stevenage, Hertfordshire
Stoke-on-Trent
Sunderland, Tyne and Wear
Swansea
Taff Ely, Wales
Tameside, Greater Manchester
Tamworth, Staffordshire
Torfaen, Wales
Waltham Forest, Outer London
Wansbeck, Northumberland
Wigan, Greater Manchester
Wakefield, West Yorkshire
Worcester
Wrexham Maelor, Wales
Ynys Mon, Wales

Source: Department of the Environment, Welsh Office and Scottish Office.

BRITAIN'S CHEAPEST AREAS

The local authorities common to both tables.

Barnsley, South Yorkshire
Easington, Durham
Gateshead, Tyne and Wear
Great Grimsby, Humberside
Kingston-upon-Hull
Manchester
Scunthorpe, Humberside
Sunderland, Tyne and Wear
Wansbeck, Northumberland

There is another side to having the right address. For anyone who can afford to choose where to live, quality of life has become a prime motivation. Peace of mind, as much as prosperity, is now the dream of many people wanting to escape crime, pollution, poor schools and traffic jams. Their attitudes have resulted in an upheaval in the relative desirability of different areas. By such a measure, it is clear that the good life exists on both sides of the north-south divide. As the *Economist* magazine concluded at the start of the Major era: 'People like having cash in their pockets, but many, including the well-off, believe that the quality of life in Britain – the cleanliness of its cities, the quality of its education, the punctuality of its trains – has been deteriorating, is deteriorating and should be improved.'

The Glasgow Quality of Life Group, a team of academics, has been at the forefront of calculating the best places to live and work. In 1989 it published a list of Britain's 72 biggest cities, ranking them according to their quality of life. The findings challenge the widely held view that the south and southeast of England are the best places to live. Overall, the most desirable areas were in Scotland, the north of England, Wales and the southwest. The least desirable region was the Midlands.

THE BEST AND WORST LARGE TOWNS AND CITIES TO LIVE IN

Best	Worst
Edinburgh	Sandwell
Exeter	Birmingham
Aberdeen	Wolverhampton
Halifax	Walsall
Dundee	Nottingham
York	Dudley
Cambridge	Mansfield
Plymouth	Slough
Swansea	Coventry
Southend	Manchester

Source: Glasgow Quality of Life Group, 1989.

Two years later the same group declared Perth, the 'fair city' of Tayside, the best place to live in Britain in the 1990s. The ancient capital of Scotland, setting for one of Sir Walter Scott's historical novels, came top in a comprehensive study of 145 towns and cities with populations between 100,000 and 200,000. People in the Midlands were once again most likely to get the worst of both worlds. 'They are trapped between the private wealth-creation centres of the south and places in the north that may benefit from government aid,' the researchers concluded.

THE BEST AND WORST DISTRICTS

Best	Worst
Perth and Kinross	Gedling (Arnold)
Kyle and Carrick (Ayr)	Rushcliffe (West Bridgford)
South Lakeland (Kendal)	Ashfield (Kirkby in Ashfield)
Dacorum (Hemel Hempstead)	Epping Forest
Basingstoke and Deane	Elmbridge (Walton-on-Thames)
Northampton	Mansfield
York	Monklands (Coatbridge)
Eastleigh	Broxtowe (Beeston)
Exeter	Spelthorne (Staines)
South Norfolk	Newark and Sherwood

Source: Glasgow Quality of Life Group, 1991.

In one of its earliest studies the Quality of Life Group conceded that one of the motivating factors for undertaking such comparisons was to satisfy public curiosity. The group said: 'The most basic reason for rating places in terms of their quality of life would appear to be to satisfy the basic human desire of "keeping up with the Joneses" or, rather, of knowing how well or badly one is "keeping up with the Joneses".' The research, using a representative national sample of more than 2,000 people, identified their main concerns as health care, crime, the cost of living, pollution, shopping facilities, education, house prices, wage levels and the natural beauty of the area.

For big cities, crime played a key part in diminishing the overall quality of life. The cost of living and pollution exacerbated negative scores. Edinburgh ranked as the best city in terms of health provision, sports and leisure facilities, as well as being highly ranked for education and short travel-to-work times. Exeter fared well because it had the least polluted environment and was highly ranked for sports and leisure facilities. It also had one of the lowest costs of living and one of the best transport networks. Perth was

commended for its excellent education and health facilities: it had
the best pupil-teacher ratio and a high number of doctors per head
of population. After health care, freedom from the fear of burglary
and mugging was the most important factor listed by people when
asked about their ideal place to live. While the Perth and Kinross
district reports about 1,000 crimes a month, most are minor offences
and residents feel safe in their homes.

By contrast, the cities of the southeast do not generally have a high
quality of life, according to researchers. Their poor performance
reflects the high cost of living, inflated property prices and poor
social facilities, such as health, education, sports and leisure.
London ranked close to the bottom: although it appears to benefit
from a concentration of cultural and other facilities, the picture is
very different when you take into account the size of the population.
In fact, Londoners fare worse than those in smaller cities, whether in
the southeast or elsewhere in Britain.

An alternative middle class is emerging. More and more people
are opting for the good life, abandoning career prospects and
apparently sacrificing social status. The friends they leave behind
think they are eccentric, although they may harbour secret
feelings of envy. The migrants are blazing a trail and opening
up a new frontier of 'honeypot' towns and cities. The scale of the
social change and the potency of the new middle-class values are
already making a significant impression. Between 1981 and 1989,
London lost more people by outward migration than anywhere
else (down by 224,500), followed by other big cities such as
Birmingham (down by 58,900) and Liverpool (down by
54,700). Among the biggest losers were Bristol (down by
33,000) and Kingston-upon-Hull (down by 35,400). Outward
migration from the southeast rose from an annual average of
5,000 in the mid-1980s to nearly 60,000 by the end of the decade.
At the same time, Scotland saw a reversal in migration trends:
from a net loss of population of more than 24,000 in 1987 to a net
gain of 13,500 by 1990.

Some of these migrants have turned their backs on the urban rat
race simply to pursue a more eccentric lifestyle. The majority,
however, are the new middle class: the managers and professionals
on the way up. Many of these trendsetters are self-employed or are
'tele-commuters' taking full advantage of new technology. They are
forging a new pecking order of the best places to live, one which is

133

far different from that ordained by the property snobs of the old order. They are the new class warriors.

Nightmare on negative equity street is being played out in a road near you. Nowhere have the pressures of downward mobility been as great as in the housing market. The losers have been those property buyers, mainly young couples, who purchased at the height of the housing boom in 1989 and have seen the value of their investment plummet. Many are sitting on assets worth less than their mortgages, and cannot afford to move because they would lose thousands of pounds that they owe to their building society or bank. The winners are the ones who sold to the losers: they have climbed the social ladder by making a move at the right time and scooping windfall profits beyond their dreams.

The proportion of homeowners with negative equity rose by a fifth in 1993 as house prices continued to fall in many parts of the country. It is estimated that more than 1 million households are caught in the negative equity trap. According to research by the Joseph Rowntree Foundation, more than a quarter of recent house-buyers – nearly half of them in their early 20s – owe more on their mortgages than they could raise by selling their homes. The average amount of negative equity has risen from £3,600 in October 1991 to £4,400 in 1992 and £4,800 by October 1992. Younger buyers have suffered most: with lower savings, they have been forced to borrow a greater proportion of the value of their homes.

The problem has been greatest, and grew quickest, in the south. Of those who bought their houses between 1988 and 1991 in London and the southeast, more than four in 10 are in negative equity; more than three in 10 face the problem in East Anglia, the East Midlands and the southwest. By contrast, fewer than one in 10 in the same group in Wales and the north of England have negative equity, and only one in 20 buyers in Scotland could not pay off their mortgages by selling their houses.

The problem is so acute in the southeast that experts predict that even if property prices went up by 25% over the next few years, many householders in the region would still be trapped. Some analysts forecast that negative equity will continue into the next century. John Wriglesworth, of stockbrokers UBS Phillips & Drew was among the first to identify the phenomenon. 'It is not the traditionally worst-off who have suffered. It has affected the high-flyers and first-time buyers most, and has been a big jolt to the middle class,' he said.

Negative equity has had its political fallout, causing widespread disillusion among voters in the Tory heartlands of the south. The people of Huntingdon, John Major's Cambridgeshire constituency, have been among the most unfortunate homeowners in Britain: the value of their properties fell by an average of £54 a day in the four years after 1988. Towns such as Peterborough and Norwich in East Anglia have seen some of the biggest falls. In Swindon at least half the houses on many new residential estates were worth less than their mortgages in 1992. The Wiltshire town, with its concentration of high-technology companies, was previously hailed as Europe's fastest-growing urban area. Experts once said it was in danger of 'over-employment' and swallowing surrounding villages.

All that has changed. At Bramwell Close, a smart estate of 61 two- and three-bedroomed houses built between 1988 and 1990, 55% of home-owners were living in houses worth less than their mortgages. With no possibility of moving for several years, the residents were forced to delay having families or build extensions on their homes. 'The strain on our marriage has been unbelieveable,' said one, a computer sales manager. 'Everyone was desperate to lend us money and like mugs we took it.' Things could be worse, however. Negative equity has put on hold the aspirations of thousands of home-owners, but it has not been sufficient to drive them down the social ladder. This indignity is reserved for the 'repossessed' – those who have had to surrender their homes because they can no longer meet the mortgage payments. Socially, they are worse off than the meanest council tenant. The repossessed tried to espouse middle-class values, and failed. Their class position is in a spiral.

Official statistics underplay the number of people heading for the social oblivion that is no longer owning your own home. In 1989, when property prices were at their highest, about 50,000 court orders were made for repossessions; two years later, in the middle of the economic slump, 140,000 orders were made, an increase of 180%. Although the number of repossessions has dropped since then, they are still running at a high level – about 30,000 every three months. Behind the statistics, thousands more live in quiet dread that it will be their turn next.

For all its financial risks, however, home-ownership remains a prize that Britons believe is worth striving for. A 1993 study by

Shelter, the housing charity, confirmed that across the social spectrum the vast majority of people remain wedded to the idea of owning their homes. Nearly eight in 10 respondents said they would prefer to pay for their housing with a mortgage compared with one in eight (12%) who favoured renting from a local authority, and just one in 100 who wanted to rent privately. Only financial worries about unemployment, repossession and inability to meet mortgage repayments were given as reasons why a minority would be content to rent.

The home you own is as important as your job in determining your social position. It is not only a status symbol: it can improve your quality of life and earn you money at the same time. In fact, over the years, it can generate more disposable cash for you than a lifetime of work. Like no other possession, it embodies the achievements of the past and ambitions for the future. You cannot be secure in your class ranking unless you are winning the battle on the home front.

CHAPTER EIGHT

THE NEW CONSUMERS

NEVER has such a wide variety of material possessions been so sought after by people of all classes. What we buy, probably more than anything else, defines where we stand in society. In short, it is what is now commonly called 'lifestyle', an invention of the late 20th century that is largely moulded by personal wealth and the exercising of a seemingly infinite number of individual choices. People are grouped according to what they wear, where they shop, what they eat and drink, how they speak, even their attitudes and sense of humour. Lifestyle is not merely a symptom of class: it is a creator of class. It can belie your occupational classification: there is no automatic link between the job you do and the life you lead, your possessions, your tastes or cultural pursuits. For this reason, more than any other, a holistic approach is needed to determine your class. It also helps to answer a crucial question: how can you 'style' your life to climb the class ladder?

Napoleon has ultimately been proved wrong in his description of Britain as 'a nation of shopkeepers'. Britain is now a nation of high-spending shoppers. In 1992, consumers spent a remarkable £440 billion, an average of £8,000 for every man, woman and child in the country; the amount is 16 times more than the money put aside in savings and half as much again, in real terms, than was spent in 1976. Of course, some people have a greater ability to make a greater number of consumer choices simply because they have more money: the wealthiest fifth of households account for nearly half of all consumer spending and saving. The poorest fifth are restricted to only one-twentieth of the consumer market, a relatively small slice of the cake. But because the cake is getting ever bigger, the freedom of choice of many more consumers is also expanding.

The big spenders who set the pace for the rest obviously include those in the highest-paid jobs. But they are not the only ones. The old-fashioned hierarchy of occupational groupings is not replicated in spending patterns in the consumer market. Although the occupational As, with average annual household incomes of £39,000, spend the most, they do not dominate across the board. For example, it is not the As who spend proportionately the most on electrical goods, it is the Bs; it is not the As who spend the most on beer, it is the Cs; and it is certainly not the As who spend the most on tobacco, it is the Es, particularly the unemployed. In the world of do-it-yourself, it is the self-employed, many of whom are manually skilled, who stand out.

Essex Man, one of Britain's most strident class warriors with his mobile phone, Ford Escort XR3i and 'loadsamoney' mentality, is a doyen among consumers. He is defined entirely by a peculiar lifestyle and set of attitudes that prevail well beyond the boundaries of a single county. Although he took a beating in the recession and with the passing of Thatcherism, he remains a model, however much maligned by the old middle class, of the aspirational way of life. Simon Heffer, the journalist who identified the emergence of such a brash anti-hero, says it is only the ignorant who look down upon Essex Man: 'Those who sneer at self-improvement fall into two categories: those who forget that, at some time in the past, they or their forebears self-improved; and those who lack the drive, ability, intelligence and wit to improve, and resent others who have those qualities.'

Material possessions are strangely imbued with a 'language' that classifies their owners. Yuppies, the young professional cousins of Essex Man, made their name in the 1980s with the Big Bang in the City, but they were essentially a creation of an even bigger bang at the heart of society. Their hallmark was an upwardly mobile life of conspicuous consumption: flaunting their good fortune by driving Porsches as brightly coloured as their braces, gulping Dom Perignon whenever in public and turning 'power-dressing' into a uniform. After maturing into thirtysomethings, their consumption may have become less conspicuous, but it is still the defining characteristic.

Just as the traditional occupational groups are crude caricatures of class, so these media inventions are over-simplified generalisations. There is more to Essex Man than a mobile phone, more to a yuppie than a Porsche, and more to a thirtysomething than a job in advertising. Lifestyle, like class, is partly a product of your previous circumstances, but changes with your age and ambitions. It is an everyday expression of your past, present and future. Middle-aged couples with teenage children and average household incomes of more than £29,000 emerge as among the biggest spenders; childless under-40s spend the most on clothes, meals out and entertainment, while over-50s who have yet to retire account for the biggest outlay on holidays, gardening and savings. Those in their 30s spend proportionately more on housing and children's clothing than any other age group; under-35 'singletons' are the peak purchasers of televisions, video recorders and hi-fi equipment.

How much you spend and what you spend it on can vary according to which part of the country you live in. Cultural influences and differences in the cost of living increase the number of permutations in the spectrum of lifestyles. Although household income is greatest in London, people in the capital are by no means the highest spenders across the whole range of goods and services. Households in the northwest spend proportionately more than those elsewhere in the country on men's clothing, beer and luxury goods; households in the southwest spend the most on cars, while the Welsh are by far the biggest savers; those in Northern Ireland are second to none in their spending on children's clothing, toys and bicycles.

THE CASH PEOPLE HAVE TO SPEND

Area	Disposable income per head
Southeast	£8,043
Scotland	£7,103
East Anglia	£6,928
East Midlands	£6,776
Northwest	£6,742
Southwest	£6,693
Yorkshire/Humberside	£6,581
West Midlands	£6,489
North	£6,454
Northern Ireland	£6,112
Wales	£6,059
United Kingdom	£7,071

Source: *Regional Trends*, 1993.

For millions of people, shopping is a way of life. From camcorders and Cartier watches to satellite dishes and saunas, you can quickly slide down the social pecking order if you do not maintain a full portfolio of lifestyle accessories. The growth of the middle class has been made possible by the development of 'egalitarian capitalism', the rapid spread of once-exclusive possessions to a mass market of ordinary consumers. Twenty-five years ago, ownership of a colour television set made you the envy of your neighbours, but not any more. The same goes for a telephone, washing machine and even central heating. Household gadgets, which started life beyond the pockets of most people, have quickly become affordable because of technological improvements in production and the desire of manufacturers to cash in on economies of scale. In the fast-moving consumer markets of the 1990s nothing ever remains exclusive long enough to stay the preserve of an élite.

Given the array of goods and services on offer, it is what you choose to buy and what you choose not to spend your money on that signals your class. Significantly, the wealthiest one-fifth of households spends substantially more on education, pensions and their homes than any other group. They invest in the future to secure their position in society. They are not just class visitors who live for the moment. Similarly, they are not consumers who merely indulge in a series of one-off purchases just because they have come into a windfall or the money happens to be at hand.

Every purchase, however, transmits its own class message. Satellite dishes are among the latest products to create a divide between the haves and have-nots, but are nevertheless of dubious class credentials. In some cases, it is better to be among the have-nots. Cable television is a different matter: it has been installed in largely affluent areas such as the London boroughs of Westminster and Croydon, and has more cachet because it is less conspicuous. There are some possessions that are sure signs that their owners are unquestionably well up the social ladder. Not even the most eccentric working-class family would have a Rolex watch, tennis court in the back garden, or any boat bigger than a sailing dinghy.

EVERY HOME SHOULD HAVE ONE

Percentage of households with:	1972	1976	1981	1985	1992
Telephone	42	54	75	81	89
Colour television	–	49	74	86	97
Video recorder	–	–	–	31	70
Home computer	–	–	–	13	21
Compact disc player	–	–	–	–	27
Washing machine	66	71	78	81	90
Dishwasher	–	–	4	6	15
Central heating	37	48	59	69	84
Car (one or more)	52	56	59	62	68

Source: GfK Marketing Services, 1992.

Egalitarian capitalism is nowhere more in evidence than in the spread of mobile phones, which Norman Lamont, the former chancellor, branded 'one of the greatest scourges of modern life' after yuppie conversations disturbed quiet dinners at his favourite London restaurant. The phones have rapidly become everyday tools of self-employed tradesmen and travelling salesmen in company cars. Launched less than a decade ago, the mobile networks already have nearly 2 million subscribers. By the end of 1994 they expect to have at least 2.5 million users and 5.6 million by the year 2000, equivalent to one in 10 of the population. 'It has become the plumber's mate,' says a spokesman for Vodafone, one of the cellular operators.

Sometimes, ownership – or the semblance of it – is more important than what is owned, or the value it offers. It can add enviable gloss to your life, without others scrutinising too closely what practicable benefit or substance it provides. Timeshare is a prime example. Whether or not you actually own the freehold to that villa in Tenerife is irrelevant – you behave as if you do, at least for two weeks of the year. Hard-sell tactics by get-rich-quick salesmen have found no shortage of 'get-class-quick' customers. The number of timeshare owners rocketed during the Thatcher years: in 1980 there were fewer than 20,000 in Britain, while today the figure is more than 250,000. The Canaries are the timeshare capital, accounting for about one-third of all British owners, although it is closely followed by Spain, Portugal and Britain itself. Timeshare owners have aspirations beyond their means: in pursuit of cut-price upward mobility, they pay an average of £7,000 to entitle them to spend the same week in the same month at the same villa for the next 25 years. For an additional fee they can join a members' exchange scheme to swap accommodation around the world. They pay through the nose to acquire the aura of jet-setting, cosmopolitan travellers while actually getting little more than a self-catering package holiday. The typical profile of an owner is an occupational A, B or C1 aged over 45, with grown-up children and earning a minimum of £15,000 a year. 'Ownership is an obvious attraction, but there is also that combination of independence and knowing where you are going that appeals to many people,' says Jane Evans, of RCI Europe, a timeshare exchange company.

Food shopping, routine as it may seem, is one of the most revealing class activities. Everybody does it: whether you buy Tesco's own-label sardines or smoked salmon from Harrods Food Hall, you are branded by where you or your family shop. Even something as trivial as the plastic shopping bag you carry, emblazoned with the store's name, advertises your status. The most important achievement of the big supermarkets, however, has been to disseminate middle-class tastes to the rest of the population. After all, anyone can now buy smoked salmon at their local Tesco's.

Nevertheless, social differences exist between all the high street shops, and are particularly marked between supermarkets. Such is their social cachet that some cut-price own-labels are no longer the embarrassment they once were. Not so long ago it was a crucial part of preparing for a dinner party to decant the supermarket wine; now, if the label on the bottle is the right one, a Sainsbury Cabernet Sauvignon or a Waitrose Rioja, it can be prominently displayed on the table. It is widely thought that Sainsbury, above all other supermarkets, is where the middle classes are to be found. However, the highest proportion of occupational As and Bs – three in 10 – use Tesco for their main shopping; the proportion for Sainsbury is fewer than one in six, about the same as for Safeway. But the spending patterns of sophisticated consumers have become much more complex. The heyday of one-stop shopping is on the way out. What is the point in paying premium prices for mundane household goods that could never bestow any status at all? How could it matter whether you buy bleach from Waitrose or Kwik Save? The most cost-effective way to make an impression is to pick-and-mix.

Upwardly mobile consumers are likely to be top-up shoppers, visiting their nearest superstores for everyday necessities, but crossing town to drop in on Marks & Spencer or Sainsbury for something that bit special: salmon *en croûte*, fresh lychees and even handmade birthday cakes by Jane Asher's private company. Nearly half of all As and Bs use Marks & Spencer for 'secondary' food shopping; the proportion for Sainsbury is more than one in three (35%).

WHO SHOPS WHERE

	AB	C1	C2	D	E
			Percentages		
Tesco	30	16	17	20	7
Sainsbury	17	24	16	12	9
Safeway	15	12	9	5	5
Kwik Save	2	5	10	12	21

Source: BMRB/Mintel, 1994.

It is not only where you shop that counts, it is what you put in your trolley. Take drinks. At one time, champagne was an upper-class drink, but now you can buy it in supermarkets for £9.99 a bottle. It is the ultimate example of how an icon of the old élite has been downgraded by its popularity among the middle class, many of whom were initially attracted by its apparent exclusivity. Port remains an upper-class drink provided it is consumed after a meal and is not mixed with anything, even ice. A good single malt whisky is both upper class and middle class, although blended whisky is drunk by almost anybody. Gin comes closest to the notion of a 'classless' drink; from the gin palaces of Hogarth to the country clubs of the British Raj, it has been popular at various times across the whole spectrum of society. Today, it is as likely to be drunk as an aperitif in a gentleman's club in St James's as it is to be downed all night at a hen party for office workers from Slough.

It is wine, however, that is the house drink of the new middle classes. They are the self-confident connoisseurs of a new vintage. For them, it is perfectly proper to serve a New World white or Bulgarian red at a dinner party; for the old guard, nothing can compete with a fine claret or full-bodied Burgundy, particularly if it

143

comes from an illustrious importer in Belgravia rather than Sains-bury's vintage collection. The middle classes are moving in, even on beer. Their tastes and desires for exclusivity have created a new pecking order that includes cask-conditioned real ale and expensive imported 'designer' beers such as San Miguel (from Spain) and Michelob (from the United States). Class-conscious drinkers are to be found drinking not out of a glass, but directly from the bottle, and often with a wedge of lime forced into the neck to let everyone see they know what they are doing.

Tea is Britain's number one beverage, but it is far from classless. Earl Grey, flavoured with bergamot, and Darjeeling, the 'cham-pagne of teas', are, since the advent of tea bags, an even more firmly entrenched preserve of the traditional upper classes and middle classes. Members of the working classes instinctively plump for PG Tips and TyPhoo, mixtures of stronger Kenyan and Indian teas that the middle classes sometimes refer to as 'breakfast blends'. (Only the old working class drink tea with their meals.) Coffee has soared in popularity in recent years, its appeal being greatest among upwardly mobile professionals. Espresso, Nescafé Gold Blend and decaffei-nated coffee are definitely aspirational; cappucino, Maxwell House and Irish coffee are favoured by the non-manual working class.

Beyond the necessities, there are limitless opportunities for new consumers to exercise their class discretion. John Lewis and Marks & Spencer are quintessentially middle class. So are Harrods, Self-ridges and Harvey Nichols, at least at sale time. Debenhams tries hard to be and some House of Fraser stores such as Kendals in Manchester and Rackhams in Birmingham have actually suc-ceeded. Habitat used to be, and IKEA, the Swedish furniture retailer, would like you to think it is. Jenners of Edinburgh definitely is; Woolworth, Argos and Ratners definitely are not; BhS and C & A are orthodox working class, as is Littlewoods. The Body Shop does not know what class it is, while Laura Ashley does not care what it is, provided it has pretty wild flowers printed on it.

Your wardrobe is as much a class statement as a fashion statement. For the upper classes there is a simple rule with clothing: new is vulgar, threadbare is distinguished. There is nothing that reveals where you stand in society quite so blatantly as a pristine Barbour, the protective oilskin coat synonymous with the huntin'-shootin'-fishin' fraternity. Some members of the upper class go a stage further; always keen to cling to the past, they are more than happy to wear their grandparents' clothing if any are to hand. Suits made 50 years ago by Savile Row tailors are just starting to wear in. They sport 'sensible' shoes – typically, by Church's of Northampton – and women like to be seen wearing Hermes scarves with their Barbours. Hand-made shirts from Jermyn Street in St James's are *de rigueur*.

The new élite are less preoccupied with the names of the past. As John Birt, the BBC director-general, has shown with his love of Armani suits, its members are *aficionados* of designer labels: Yves St Laurent, Pierre Cardin and Burberry sell mass-produced, ready-to-wear clothing at tailor-made prices. Successful members of the middle class have a common clothes sense: they believe first impressions are important and that they can assert themselves not by force of personality, but by the way they look. Garish braces and over-patterned silk ties, if now somewhat dated, are still used widely at work to leave a lasting impression. In women's wear, designer fashions are considerably more exclusive, with sky-high prices to match. Chanel dresses, Catherine Charles suits and Versace blouses are emblems of successful career women who have conquered in a male-dominated world. Other ambitious working women recognise the need to look the part: they dress not so much for the jobs they have, but for the jobs they want.

Working-class wear is equally distinctive, but there is a clear division between their working attire and what they put on when they 'dress up' for a night out. In general, the working classes, unlike those higher up the social ladder, pay more attention to their clothes when they are away from work. White trainers, shellsuits, grey shoes and nylon leggings are typical accessories. Top Man, Top Shop, Miss Selfridge and C & A are the labels they look for when out clothes shopping. Cloth caps, the stereotypical headwear of the working classes, have risen in status more than any other item of clothing. The fact that such an integral part of the working-class 'uniform' has been abandoned almost within a single generation is symbolic of the pace of social change and the disintegration of working-class solidarity.

The big spenders are not necessarily the old élite. There are three activities – eating out, holidays and health care – that have been transformed by upwardly mobile consumers. Even the most narrow-minded proletarian is willing to entertain the possibility that home cooking is not always the best, and the local seaside resort is not the only place to visit on holiday. The arrival of ethnic restaurants in every town and city has overturned previous notions about where and when we eat: going for an 'Indian' or a 'Chinese' has made eating out a habit. Since 1987, the catering industry has enjoyed one of the most spectacular increases in consumer spending, rising by £7 billion or nearly 30% in real terms; one-fifth of all the money we spend on food each week goes on dining out. Going to a restaurant is now commonplace: it is the venue you choose that sets you apart. The new middle classes like nothing more than to be seen in a 'fashionable' restaurant, preferably with a 'superchef' as owner. You invariably know that you are in the right establishment by menus that have 'dates of creation' beside each dish, as well as the absence of a salt-cellar on the table. The quality of the food, however, is secondary, and a £200 dinner for two can sometimes disappoint. Moreover, exclusivity is a fragile commodity, particularly when expense-account lunches and dinners are part of everyday working life for even the moderately well-off.

After your house and car, holidays are the biggest recurrent item of expenditure. Choosing a holiday is a big decision: you talk about it, think about it and study brochures almost all year round. The end result, what you decide to do and where, is an ingredient of your class. In the 1930s an estimated 1.5 million people set off on foreign holidays each year, but it was only after the Second World War, when the concept of 'holidays with pay' was largely accepted by employers, that the market expanded beyond the established middle class. Package travel and charter flights made holidays to exotic locations affordable for the masses; by 1992 the British went on a total of 23 million foreign holidays, nearly three-quarters of them taken in European Union countries. About one-tenth were spent in North America, and a similar proportion were even further afield.

The range of holidays available has never been greater, but your social status is reflected in which you select. The seriously rich move around in a clique each year from one fashionable resort to another. To earn their patronage, a paradise island or Alpine village invariably requires the endorsement of a minor royal's visit. By contrast, the working classes go almost anywhere they can get a good rate for the pound. Slowly, however, they have become more adventurous in their choice of destination: families from Dundee to Dudley now travel to Greece, America and Thailand when 10 years

ago they kept to Majorca and the Algarve. The comforting familiarity of places such as New Zealand and the English-speaking parts
of Canada has turned them into seasoned long-haul travellers. The
middle classes simply go to France. The type of accommodation can
be crucial: the middle classes would never dream of staying in a
caravan, but it is acceptable to camp, particularly on foreign soil.
Hotels are favoured by the upper and working classes, whereas the
middle classes, who pride themselves on their independence and
self-reliance, often prefer self-catering in an apartment or villa. For
the family holiday in France, they opt for a *gîte*, a term that has
become the all-embracing description for any rented accommodation, no matter how ordinary, in any vaguely rural setting. Winter
skiing marks a class threshold that separates the masses from those
for whom holidays are part of a social calendar. First you have to be
able to afford at least two holidays a year, and time spent on the piste
is more expensive than almost anywhere else. While the rich and
famous jet between Gstaad and Aspen, the middle classes head for
the Alpine slopes of France and Italy – the Austrian Alps are booked
only as a last resort. The piste is the place to perform, and not the
disco dance floor of the 'après-ski'.

Nowadays, only politicians pretend to be embarrassed about
'going private' for health care. Even more than private education,
medical insurance is within the reach of ordinary people for whom
the National Health Service was created. Although more than a
quarter (27%) are professionals, as many as one in 25 are manual
workers. In public, the NHS is defended as one of Britain's greatest
institutions; in private, millions of people are taking the precaution
of medical insurance to maintain the same status when they are ill as
when they are healthy. In 1970, under 2 million people, less than 4%
of the population, were covered by Bupa and other private insurers;
since then, the number has more than trebled to 6.3 million, or
nearly one in eight people. Like a company car, it is a perk of your
job that is a measure of the esteem in which you are held at work.
Less than half the people covered pay for it themselves, while the
rest have insurance that is paid wholly or in part by their employers.
There are big regional differences: as many as one in five living in
the southeast are covered by private insurance compared with less
than one in 20 in the north of England.

Of all the unhealthy vices, smoking is the most telling. Once
popular among all classes, it has fallen out of fashion because of

essentially middle-class concerns about personal health. Money that used to be spent on nicotine is now spent on sojourns at expensive health farms and twice-weekly visits to fitness centres. By the beginning of the 1990s, less than a third of men smoked, compared with more than half 20 years earlier. There has been a similar decline in smoking among mature women. In 1992, fewer than one in seven occupational As smoked, compared with nearly two in five Ds and Es; while 14% of professional women smoke at the start of pregnancy, the proportion among unskilled women is more than four times higher at 61%.

WHO THE SMOKERS ARE

	Men, %	Women,%
As	14	13
Bs	23	21
C1s	25	27
C2s	34	31
Ds	39	35
Es	42	35

Source: *General Household Survey*, 1992.

What you do in your spare time reinforces your class position. The activities you pursue, as a participant or spectator, reflect where you see yourself in society. The middle classes are the clubbable classes: they are twice as likely to belong to leisure groups and voluntary organisations as almost anybody else. Being a member of a club is only a start, the first step, to ascending a new social ladder by becoming a committee member and ultimately, perhaps, the club secretary. For decades the upper classes, middle classes and working classes have each been associated with certain sports and leisure pursuits. But all this is changing in the 1990s: it is the activity that they have in common, not necessarily their class identity. The upper classes remain passionate about shooting and are obsessed with horses, whether racing them, jumping them or simply breeding them. These days, however, you are just as likely to find a Surrey businessman hunting with the hounds as a Sussex lord of the manor. Many sports that were once class-ridden, in the orthodox sense, are now pursued by members of the new élite. Conversely, it is not unknown for aristocrats to stand on the terraces at soccer matches, from where they may even catch sight of the prime minister in the stands and wealthy businessmen drinking champagne in executive boxes.

Golf is the first love of the middle classes. There are currently more than 1 million members of golf clubs, ranging from championship courses such as The Belfry and Wentworth to humble seaside links. For some of the most exclusive clubs, the waiting lists can be as long as five years. Only in Scotland has the sport retained its character as the people's game. There, a round of golf can be played on a top-class municipal course for less than £5. The high costs of membership elsewhere, plus the initial expense in purchasing all the equipment, has deterred the working classes. For the middle classes, golf is more than a game: it provides an atmosphere in which they can be at ease with their own and free to mix pleasure with business. Cricket has been less adept in protecting its status as the other great game of the middle classes, even though it has maintained the arcane exclusivity of the gentlemen's club *par excellence*, the MCC. No longer is the division simply between 'gentlemen' and 'players': the polite applause from the pavilion is now likely to be drowned by the rowdiness from the beer tents on the other side of the pitch. Athletics, some of whose greatest moments are associated with Oxbridge 'blues', is emerging as the classless sport of the 1990s. With the cost of equipment relatively low, its superstars are true meritocrats who have won gold despite, rather than because of, their backgrounds. The differences between Linford Christie, Sebastian Coe, Sally Gunnell and Fatima Whitbread are nothing compared to the similarity of their achievements.

Nowhere is clubbiness greater than in the arts, whose biggest supporters are the middle classes. And nowhere is it easier for the new élite to rub shoulders with each other and celebrities. Often combined with charitable fund-raising events or performances, their wealth buys them a place at the table. Corporate sponsorship also opens doors for executives at premieres and first-night parties, and often forces artists and writers to play to a wider audience. The Booker Prize is symbolic of the trend: it has taken literature out of the secret gardens of academe and put it on prime-time television, if only on BBC 2. The winner is guaranteed to be a bestseller in every high street in the country.

The English Season – strawberries and cream at Wimbledon,

cartwheel hats for Ascot and that 'absolutely fabulous' new Hockney at the Royal Academy summer exhibition – is at the heart of the social calendar, at whose events the spectators come to look at the spectators rather than the events themselves. The quintessential spectacle is the Royal Regatta at Henley-on-Thames held at the end of June. Rowing club blazers are obligatory and tradition calls for wicker hampers stuffed with cold chicken, caviare canapés and iced champagne. Now, however, commercial exploitation and corporate hospitality have encroached to erode the social barriers that kept out the masses. Whether it is Wimbledon or the Epsom Derby, television has given ordinary viewers the best seats on offer. Meanwhile, executives of multinational companies, privatised utilities and financial institutions have infiltrated the traditional audiences, buying up the most sought-after vantage points and commissioning the finest catering to entertain clients.

'The mass of the rich and the poor,' George Orwell wrote in his 1933 classic, *Down and Out in Paris and London*, 'are differentiated by their incomes and nothing else, and the average millionaire is only the average dishwasher dressed in a new suit.' In his characteristically phlegmatic way, the Eton-educated Orwell failed to grasp the full significance of social snobbery and its relationship to class. Your precise position in the pecking order can depend on an awareness of cultural icons, and knowledge of who and what really counts. Whether rightly or wrongly – and regardless of personal wealth, property and career success – fine-tuning your class ranking can come down to the airs and graces you adopt as well as your behaviour to others, the vocabulary you use and even your sense of humour.

Which newspaper you read is one of the most reliable class indicators. It is said, somewhat cruelly, that the *Daily Telegraph* is read by people who think they should run the country, the *Guardian* by people who want to run the country, *The Times* by people who actually do run the country – and the *Sun* by people who do not care who is running the country, provided they have big breasts! Such class stereotypes, however, are gradually disappearing: the *Sun*, with a circulation of 4 million, has nearly three times as many occupational As and Bs as *The Times* and the *Financial Times*; many of its readers can be spotted on commuter trains in the southeast, including businessmen catching up on the latest scandal before throwing their copies in the bin and buying a quality broadsheet suitable for the office. More than a quarter of those who read *The Times* and *FT* are C1s, far removed from the political and financial élite that both newspapers cater for. A further one in 20 are unskilled or semi-skilled workers such as road-sweepers, bus conductors and refuse collectors. Even the *News of the World* attracts more than 300,000 As and Bs, more than any Sunday quality broadsheet except the *Sunday Times*.

THE NEWSPAPERS WE READ

National dailies – Percentages				
A	**B**	**C1**	**C2**	**D/E**
The Times 18	42	26	8	6
Financial Times 15	43	28	9	5
Guardian 7	46	30	8	5
Daily Telegraph 13	37	31	12	7
Independent 10	38	31	12	9
Daily Mail 5	24	36	20	16
Daily Express 4	21	33	26	17
Today 1	15	29	29	26
Daily Mirror 1	8	22	33	36
Daily Record 1	8	25	30	37
Sun 1	7	22	33	39
Star 0	6	19	35	40

National Sundays – Percentages				
Sunday Times 13	40	29	10	8
Scotland on Sunday 7	46	34	7	7
Observer 8	44	28	10	10
Independent on Sunday 11	40	34	8	8
Sunday Telegraph 12	36	31	15	7
Sunday Express 5	22	34	21	17
Mail on Sunday 4	23	36	21	16
Sunday Mail 2	9	24	29	36
People 1	9	25	31	35
Sunday Mirror 1	9	23	33	35
Sunday Sport 1	9	16	33	40
News of the World 1	8	22	33	37

Source: *National Readership Survey*, April 1993–September 1993.

From *Coronation Street* and *Casualty* to the wildlife documentaries of David Attenborough and the BBC *Nine O'Clock News*, every television programme has its own target audience. Whether on commercial television or the BBC, the ratings war is largely a question of class: broadcasters aim at attracting a relatively small number of high-class viewers or they go for a mass audience heavy with Ds and Es. Either way, popular assumptions can be misleading: *EastEnders*, for example, has one of the biggest audiences of As and Bs on British television, accounting for one in seven of the soap opera's followers. Similarly, *The Bill*, the downmarket police series on ITV, attracts 2 million As and Bs, or 15% of a 13 million audience. BBC1, with its daily schedules dominated by light entertainment and middle-brow dramas, beats Channel 4 in the race for viewers in the top two occupational groups; it also has a smaller proportion of Ds and Es. Unsurprisingly, ITV is the most downmarket television network, with nearly four in 10 viewers from the bottom two occupational groups; BBC2 is the most exclusive with nearly one in five viewers (18%) being As or Bs. An analysis in November 1993 by David Graham & Associates, an independent television information service, revealed that *Casualty*, BBC1's gory hospital drama, was the most successful programme in its appeal across the social spectrum: it had more A and B viewers than any other programme (2.6 million) and among the highest number of Ds and Es (5 million). The findings show that people of all classes are as eclectic in their viewing habits as they are in their lifestyles.

Ever since George Bernard Shaw's *Pygmalion*, the social importance of speech has been widely recognised. Even the way you say the word 'class' can, in itself, say a lot about your class. Is it class as in 'farce', or class as in 'lass'? From the confident tones of a public school accent to the nasal drone of a Brummie voice, the way we speak can be an obvious distinguishing mark. The difference today is that accents that were once unfashionable no longer count against you. Indeed, some country accents can be a positive advantage in helping to make an impression. Class distinctions in the words people use really came into the open only in the mid-1950s when Nancy Mitford provoked a furious debate after writing about the characteristics of the English aristocracy. Mitford, championing the views of a Birmingham university professor, argued that it was solely by their language that the upper classes could be distinguished, since they were neither richer nor better educated than anybody else. Thus, U and non-U speech was born. For example, 'notepaper', 'teacher' and 'perfume' were all deemed non-U, while 'writing paper', 'schoolteacher' and 'scent' were approvingly accepted as U.

Many of these judgements are antiquated, although some important relics remain. Common speech has undergone dramatic change in recent times, largely due to the influence of television. Successful people, such as Jonathan Ross, Alan Sugar and Janet Street-Porter, have made it to the top because of – rather than despite – their refusal or inability to mimic the public school accent. Estuary English, rooted in the southeast of England and typified by Ken Livingstone, Nigel Kennedy and Lord Tebbit, is so prevalent that experts forecast it could become the new standard spoken English. Even the young royals, spurning the anachronisms of the 'Queen's English', have taken to assuming a more 'street-wise' accent, a peculiar mixture of Sloane-speak and cockney. Only the Scottish upper classes have striven to preserve the past: despite their love of Highland dress and ancient Gaelic ceremonies, they continue to be easily identified by their impeccable English accents; those who have moved south of the border have the advantage of a Scottish accent that is as classless as any you can have in England. George Orwell once declared that the 'sinking' middle classes had nothing to lose but their aitches. However, no would-be members of the new élite would feel the need to speak English as it is spoken by the Queen; more than likely, they would aim at adopting a hybrid of the accents of those they aspire to join. Social success is no longer dependent on the way you speak.

CHAPTER NINE

*I*N THE FAST LANE . . . OR MONTEGO MAN?

*I*T is a potent display of success. To the rest of the world, the car you drive can say more about your class than which school you attended, what you do for a living or even where you live. From the office to the supermarket, your car is a focus for your prosperity, aspirations and taste. The image is one of a purring, or stuttering, beast tethered outside your home, confirming whether you have made your mark. Within a three-dimensional view of class, what you drive and why provides important clues to your social standing; nowhere else is the spirit of one-upmanship as prevalent.

More than any other consumer product, the car is a paradigm of egalitarian capitalism that allows everyone a share of material wealth. No longer the exclusive toys of a wealthy élite, there are now more than 23 million cars on our roads. In 1972, only about half the households in Britain ran a car, compared with more than two-thirds 20 years later; over the same period, the number of households with more than one car leapt from fewer than one in 10 to nearly a quarter. The famous saying that 'you can have any colour you like as long as it's black' is no longer appropriate: modern technology has transformed conveyor-belt mass production so that there are more models than ever to choose from. Aspiring Britons, driven by the urge to 'trade up' every three or four years, are taking advantage of this new level of choice; they see cars not just as performing a utilitarian function, but as a means of making a bold public statement about their class position.

Most men, and many women, are passionate about their cars, whether a gleaming new Mercedes or customised Alfa-Romeo built in the 1970s. They spend more on them – approximately £14 billion in 1991 – than on clothing, fuel, holidays or maintenance of their homes. To satisfy their seemingly insatiable thirst for the latest models, there are at least 130 different car magazines on sale, plus countless newspaper articles and television programmes. Regardless of this fascination, people choose cars with a particular purpose in mind, whether it is for short journeys to the office, school and shops, or racing up and down the M1 every day. But behind every choice, there is a class meaning. Each make and model carries its own connotations, however subtle.

HOW MANY CARS ON THE DRIVE?

	% of households
One car	44
Two cars	20
Three or more cars	4
Total	68

Source: *General Household Survey*, 1992.

It is no longer a question of whether or not you drive – more than 30 million people hold licences – the important thing now is what you drive and how much it is worth. The marque is all important in determining what you want your car to say about you. Aspirational motorists are intuitively aware of this: in the 1993 *Lex Report on Motoring*, a significant minority described their car as 'an extension of themselves reflecting their personality, status or success'. This view was particularly high among those aged between 17 and 34, those with cars less than three years old, or with company cars.

Cars offer almost everybody the chance to buy status. Unlike the closed society of the old élite, with their emphasis on breeding and the old boy network, the new social pecking order is rooted in personal wealth. It works rather like a voucher system: you hand over your cash and in return you are immediately hoisted up the class ladder. You come to be defined, at least away from your home and workplace, by what you drive. As one BMW dealer put it: 'We get all kinds of people in here, from all different backgrounds. But when they leave the showroom with a brand new 3-Series, they are all the same. They are all BMW owners.'

Exclusivity – or as close as you can get to it – is the key to making your mark with the car you drive. Its age is a fundamental indicator of success. There is nothing quite so enviable, or prestigious, as a brand new vehicle: just count how many newly registered cars you see in the first week of August. Among the rest, there is a simple pecking order: the average car in Britain is nearly six years old, but anything older than three years (when it requires an MoT certificate) gradually ceases to be a status symbol and becomes just another car. Buying new, however, is no guarantee of climbing the class ladder: few people are tempted by Ladas (from Russia) and Skodas (from the Czech republic), which are among the cheapest new cars on the market, costing as little as £5,000. For many they are tainted by the image and uniformity of East European socialism: the class-conscious motorist does not give a second glance at cars that inevitably make their owners appear ordinary.

Essentially, buying a car is not a matter of keeping up with the Joneses. It is about finding new ways to be different from them. The amount you have to spend is, of course, crucial: industry figures reveal that the average value of a new car is £9,200 while a used one is substantially less, at about £3,200. Faced with a choice between a brand new Ford Escort costing nearly £10,000 and a three-year-old BMW saloon or Volvo estate at the same price, class warriors are plumping for the latter as a more cost-effective way to buy status. It is only in the £25,000-plus bracket, the big league of the Jaguar XJ6 and Mercedes E Class Coupé, that your class position can be truly elevated by what you drive. With these, you are paying a premium for exclusivity; because they are luxuries bought from disposable income, they tell the world that you are seriously rich. Just as the social order is changing, the old hierarchy of cars is in a state of flux: a Rolls-Royce or a Mercedes has a different connotation today than it did 40 years ago.

For the rest, it is the minutiae of engineering, performance and decoration that make all the difference; ever since the first executive coat-hook hanging behind the head of the Ford Sierra driver, car accessories and specifications have taken on a meaning of their own. Socially aware motorists will scrutinise the fine print of specialist car magazines comparing the different features that distinguish one model from another. To the uninitiated, two vehicles may look the same in the showroom; to the *aficionado*, only one of them has 'as standard' alloy wheels, an advanced braking system and an in-car computer. Some accessories go to ridiculous extremes:

gold-coloured wheels, mahogany and walnut fascias, huge fin-like 'spoilers'. As with all class statements, you can try too hard.

In discreet, or sometimes not-so-discreet, lettering and numbering on the rear of a vehicle, drivers advertise where they are in the car pecking order. Ghia, Turbo, 16-Valve, the list is growing every year. To those who can interpret their meaning, often cryptic enough to be in code, they specify the car's performance and standards of luxury. Aspirational motorists will settle for nothing less than a fuel injection engine – 'It gives you the edge at traffic lights' – identified by the 'i' for 'important' symbol after the engine size. A Vauxhall Cavalier SRi has only one meaning: Sales Rep Inside. BMW panders to this motoring snobbery by offering to remove the badging from car boots to conceal the model type. About one in 10 customers – some 4,000 BMW-owners – take up the offer each year. The explanation from BMW is a gem of social anthropology: 'Some people do it because they are buying a less expensive model and they want people to think it is better than it really is. Others include company bosses who want to conceal the true value of their cars from employees. One BMW may look the same as another but there may be a difference of £20,000 in the price.'

The pursuit of exclusivity has led to a dramatic rise in the trade in personalised number plates. It is the marketing of individuality. In 1992, DVLA, the Swansea-based licensing body responsible for car registrations, sold nearly 75,000 such numbers, including thousands of 'select registrations', a hybrid that allows owners to choose some but not all the letters of the registration, at a cost of £250. Classic numbers can cost substantially more – £235,000 is the current record – and are usually sold at auction. What induces motorists to part with an average of £20,000 a time to buy a personalised number, such as LINKS (for golfers), VAT69 (for whisky-lovers) and MAGIX (for illusionists)? Peter Collett, a doctor of psychology at Oxford University, says the craze is all about conspicuous waste: 'There are some who buy numbers as a mark of affection. The initials of the registration may resemble the name of the owner's first child or an army regiment. For the majority, however, it really comes down to brazen one-upmanship.'

The car market in Britain is dominated more than any other in Europe by the ultimate perk – the company car. From senior board directors of top multinationals to the most junior salesmen in a small business, it has become a finely tuned gauge of executive status.

Used widely by firms in lieu of salary to retain staff, there are more company cars per capita in Britain than France, Germany, Italy and Sweden. The perk is virtually unheard of in Japan and is equally uncommon in the United States. About half the new cars registered each year in this country – nearly 1 million vehicles in 1993 – are bought by businesses for their employees. So prevalent is the perk that you can never be sure that the driver of a high-status car is also the owner.

For the beneficiaries, the company car can be a boon: at little cost, it can transport you up the class ladder in a way that you could never have done for yourself. There are, however, pitfalls. There can be nothing more galling than feeling you have to accept the E-reg Montego estate with 90,000 miles on the clock, simply because it is a company car, with all that that means, when you would really rather have a more modest but brand new Renault Clio delivered on August 1. The company car has also created its own class structure: BP, the oil company, operated one such hierarchy at the beginning of the 1990s under which managers earning £50,000 a year had the right to choose from a range of 1.8- or 2-litre models, while those on £38,000 a year were limited to 1.6-litre models. There is a world of difference between the salesman with a fleet Vauxhall Cavalier weighed down by product samples and clocking 30,000 miles or more each year, and the executive who is presented with a TVR convertible and uses it only to visit friends in the country at weekends.

Jeremy Clarkson, the *Sunday Times* columnist and BBC TV *Top Gear* presenter, is a shrewd observer of Britain's car culture. He is critical of the company car, which he says has gone a long way to undermining our deep-seated love of cars: 'Because 50% of cars sold in Britain are bought by companies, people don't bother talking about, or ogling, cars because they have what they're given . . . Why read a car magazine when next year you'll get another Cavalier, whether you like it or not? Why aspire to a Mercedes-Benz when you know your company will never buy you one, and you don't need one anyway because you have the Vauxhall for free?'

The company car, however, has taken a pounding in recent budgets and may soon be reaching the end of the road. Firms have given employees rises of up to £10,000 a year to persuade them to give up the perk. Many businesses that were the first to embrace the company car concept in the 1960s and 1970s, largely as a way around pay freezes and high taxes, are now leading the way in abandoning it. BT, for example, has provided a cash option in recent years, while Sainsbury, the supermarket group, considered paying extra to non-drivers and staff who use their own cars. City firms, where more than half the employees automatically received company cars in the past, have followed the lead set by bigger employers. Most have offered mileage allowances on top of substantial salary 'bribes'. Advertising executives, who were showered with Porsches, Lotus Elans and Morgans in the booming 1980s, have been at the forefront of making the switch.

The budget of 1991 made company cars much more expensive for both employers and employees. Treasury figures have suggested that the value of a company car to employees ranges from just over £1,000 a year for a small car that is used extensively on business, to more than £13,000 a year for a prestige marque that is mainly for the employee's own use. The rising tax burden is undermining the value of a company car as a status symbol, and underlining the fact that there is no substitute for ownership. Relying on your job for such an important signifier of your class limits individual choice and the freedom to assert yourself in the car pecking order.

Once it was the laughing stock of Europe, a car that was equated with Red Robbo, shoddy workmanship and long waits beside motorways for the breakdown service. But all that has changed: it is now chic to buy Rover. The company, which gave birth to the lacklustre Austin Allegro and Morris Marina in its former existence as British Leyland, is increasingly fashionable in Britain as well as on the Continent. The British motorist who chooses to drive one of the latest Rover models is no longer regarded as a diehard patriot, but someone of discerning taste. And now Rover has been paid the ultimate compliment: it has been bought by BMW, one of the world's greatest quality marques, to form a powerful new alliance.

By contrast, Porsche has been humbled. The car that once epitomised high performance and status is no longer the prerequisite of the young, high-earning executive. Sales have plummeted and the marque has lost out to the new breed of Japanese sports cars and increasingly popular four-wheel drive vehicles. Porsche, which symbolised success for thousands of high-flyers, is in large part a victim of its own success. Angus MacKinnon, senior editor of *GQ*, the men's arts and style magazine, draws only one conclusion: 'The cars have lost their exclusivity because too many people have them.'

What this tale of two motor manufacturers shows is that cars today are, above all else, fashion accessories, and their 'status', like that of the people who drive them, is constantly changing. From the most expensive American sports cars to innocuous South Korean saloons, our cars are no less immune to changing tastes than the latest designer clothing or the 'in' destinations for this year's summer holiday. It was not always so. Thirty years ago, motorists were fiercely loyal to British marques, which were renowned for their reliability and elegant design, and there were few competing foreign models. By the late 1970s, the car market had been transformed: the British motor industry, typified by Rover's plight, was in crisis and manufacturers from abroad were winning market share and setting new standards of luxury and performance. In 1974 less than a third of all the cars sold (1.27 million) were imported; in 1992 more than half the total of 1.59 million new vehicles came from abroad. Britain now enjoys a wider choice of cars than any other European country. As a result, we are increasingly choosy about what we drive and more sensitive to what cars say about the people who drive them.

In a market where many models are here today and gone tomorrow, the discerning motorist must be atuned to what is 'in' and what is 'out'. To maintain your class position, you have to keep on the move. There are, however, some cars that will always attract members of a certain class and social status. An élite few, by reason of their vast expense, come within reach of only the rich and famous: Rolls-Royce, Bentley and Ferrari are among the exclusive names that epitomise wealth on wheels. Beneath them are a range of luxury mass-market cars such as BMW, Jaguar and Mercedes. They are the badges of the successful entrepreneur or highly paid professional: managing directors, lawyers, dentists and hospital consultants. The big Volvo estates and Range Rovers remain the preserve of the middle class *en famille*. These cars have attracted the type of owner who relishes green wellies in the boot, dogs in the back and flaxen-haired children with names like Piers and Olivia. But even the Volvo has suffered in recent years: although sales rose from 10,500 in 1970 to 43,000 in 1992, estate agents and salesmen are attaching themselves to the marque, undermining its well-heeled image.

As a rule, foreign makes have most cachet: 'Vorsprung durch Technik' proclaims Audi's image-conscious advertising. The reason must have something to do with the prevalence of made-in-Britain company cars, and the bad reputation this country got in the 1970s for poorly made vehicles. Anything made in Germany retains the edge, although Italian marques such as Lancia and Alfa-Romeo still possess the individuality and flair to appeal to affluent, young professionals, even though they risk spending a fortune on repairs. There is now no stigma attached to buying Japanese. With manufacturing plants based in Britain, firms such as Nissan and Toyota can justifiably claim they are more British than what many would regard as quintessential domestic marques such as Ford and Vauxhall, a strong selling point for many businesses that prefer to buy British. Japanese cars had for a long time an enviable record for reliability, but their designs were uninspiring. The cars appealed to the 'something-for-nothing' mentality of the working class because features that you often paid for on European makes came 'as standard'. Nowadays Japanese cars are state of the art and considerably more expensive. Many of their drivers are members of the new middle class, who associate the makes of Nissan and Toyota with the economic miracle of an industrial power rather than distant memories of a militaristic upstart nation.

The more expensive and flamboyant the model, the more vulnerable to the vagaries of fashion it becomes. The James Bond films of the 1960s and 1970s raised the Aston Martin DBIII, DB V and Lotus Esprit to cult status, shamelessly exploiting deep-rooted ties between cars and sexual potency. But these marques today are unlikely to be the first choice of many motorists who could afford to buy them. Likewise, the Golf GTi, Escort XR3i and Peugeot 205 have fallen out of favour since insurance premiums for 'hot hatches' rocketed in the early 1990s, and Essex Man, the conspicuous consumer of the Thatcher era, hit hard times. The new 'yuppie-mobile' is the four-wheel drive vehicle which, although designed to be used off road in remote rural areas, is favoured equally as a town run-about. Psychologists believe upwardly mobile families are attracted to the likes of the Land Rover Discovery, Renault Espace and Cherokee Jeep because they can sit higher, look over traffic and feel superior. Less flamboyant and more utilitarian than Porsches, they are better suited to the spirit of the 'classless' society. Ironically, such marques are beyond the pockets of most people, with some models starting at £20,000 or more. Classlessness does not come cheap.

According to Jeremy Clarkson, marketing executives have made a science out of pigeonholing us by what we drive: 'People who buy Jaguars take their holidays in Torquay, at the Imperial, or Scotland . . . Accountants, estate agents, lawyers and stockbrokers are BMW people. Football managers and people who own casinos have Mercedes-Benzes. Gritty northern manual labourers who started with nothing and now have two swimming pools and a wife with a fur nightie have Lexuses. Scrap-metal dealers who take their holidays in Miami have Cadillacs, and vets who go to the south of France have Volvos.' There is one marque, however, which refuses to categorise its owners. 'Buy a Saab,' says Clarkson, 'and you are saying that you don't like German engineering or Italian flair. You don't like the chrominess of American design or French chassis technology. Buy a Saab and you are eschewing all the norms.' The latest models appeal to the ranks of well-off floating voters: 'Surprisingly, they do make a statement. They say to all and sundry that you, the driver, have "no comment".'

You see them everywhere, in clapped-out Volvo estates, Morris Minors and Citroen 2-CVs (CND stickers still prominently displayed). They buy wooden toys for their children at Christmas, stay in windswept *gîtes* in Brittany for their summer holidays and will gladly tell you that they do not like cars. They are surprisingly well educated, remarkably unsuccessful and have ostentatiously renounced a 'rat race' whose starting line they never even managed to reach. Of their own free will, they have chosen to stay in the crawler lane; in the car pecking order, they languish near the bottom. Next comes *Which?* magazine readers. The consumers' bible tells its 1 million middle-class members that for the umpteenth year running it is recommending some box of a car, typically a Nissan Micra or Toyota Corolla. Dutifully, *Which?* readers go out and buy it, but no one has bothered to point out that the magazine takes little account of looks and flair, and concentrates on fuel economy, safety and whether the boot has a lip on it. Their pedestrian approach to motoring confines them to the crawler lane, if not the hard shoulder.

Of necessity, others are in a jam when it comes to buying a new or better car. The number of downwardly mobile motorists increased sharply during the recession, forced to cling on to ageing vehicles. One study found that nearly one in five had delayed the purchase of a car because of the economic climate, and more than one in 10 had no choice but to buy a second-hand replacement. Helplessly, they watch their assets depreciate, and the gap widen between the value of the decaying heap they own and the cost of a successor. It is the motoring equivalent of 'negative equity' in the housing market. Most of those who bought cars in 1989, the peak year when 2.3 million were sold, own vehicles worth no more than £2,500. They will find it difficult to make up lost ground.

Some cars are non-starters if you want to stand out from the crowd. Few, if any, would dream of actually owning a Ford Sierra, Vauxhall Cavalier or Rover Montego. They are archetypal company cars, and no one will ever believe that you chose to buy one. The same could be said of the Ford Granada, Vauxhall Astra and Rover 800. To make the right impression, you have to be judicious in your selection. The British market is dominated by three manufacturers: Ford, with nearly 22% of all new car sales, Vauxhall, with a 17% share, and Rover, with 13%. With few exceptions, their models are guaranteed to make you appear exactly the same as everybody else. Some marques can even harm your standing in the eyes of others: Lada, FSO, Hyundai and Proton. They are either the butt of jokes or so nondescript as to be invisible.

There is only one thing worse: customising your car in a vain attempt to assert your ownership and individuality. It is the garden gnome mentality. Few motorists these days take pleasure in furry dice dangling from their rear-view mirror or are amused by bumper stickers that proclaim 'My other car is a Porsche'. But as one fad disappears, so another takes its place. The latest craze among the working classes is to affix silver figurines, particularly prancing horses, to the bonnet of their cars, imitating Rolls-Royce and Jaguar. Beaded seat-covers are also part of the culture. The middle classes are more subtle, absent-mindedly leaving expired parking permits for Newmarket or Hurlingham attached to their windscreen - 'Once you've stuck them on, you can't get the bloody things off' - as well as the latest unread coffee-table book carelessly flung on to the rear shelf. The ultimate middle-class sticker is that of the National Trust, closely followed by English Heritage and the Royal Academy. However, the cultural ascendant who crosses the class boundaries is not above a EuroDisney symbol, the latest badge of the *nouveau riche*.

'The car has become an article of dress,' said Marshall McLuhan, 'without which we feel uncertain, unclad and incomplete in the urban compound.' What should aspirational motorists be 'wearing'? And which cars should be the choice of those who have already made it? Married men who retain a nostalgic hunger for singledom may crave a car that enhances their image as 'wild stallions'; wives, however, are just as likely to have the final say in choosing the family car. As a result, couples with children frequently have to settle on a compromise that disappoints both, and fails to convey their true status. Single people have greater latitude, but they, too, can get it wrong: a two-seater sports car is all very well when you are a slender 25, but is far from impressive when you try and squeeze a middle-aged paunch behind the wheel.

It is a game that anyone can play while speeding on a motorway or stuck in a traffic jam on the way to the office. In 'Spot the Stereotype', everyone has his or her own prejudices – and most of them are right:

Audi: ('the Poor Man's Merc'): *80* – Teutonic salesmen allowed to choose their own company car.
BMW: *3-Series* ('the Black Man's Wheels') – estate agents, hairdressers; *M3* – paparazzi; *5-Series* (a nearly car) – provincial solicitors, deputy managers of medium-sized companies; *7-Series* – middle-aged impresarios.
Cherokee Jeep: City solicitors, property developers with too much money.
Daihatsu: *Charade* – vicars' wives.
Ferrari: garage owners, racing-car drivers.
Fiat: *Panda* – nannies, students at redbrick universities; *Uno* (the definitive second car) grandmothers, housewives; *Tempra* – minicab drivers.
Ford: (the four-wheel Michael Barrymore, the lowest common-denominator car): *Fiesta* – clerical staff in benefit offices, nurses, supermarket checkout operators; *Escort* – factory foremen, train drivers; *Granada* – insurance salesmen on big commissions.
Honda: *Civic* – middle-aged couples from the north who took early retirement; *CRX* – middle-aged gays, timeshare salesmen; *Prelude* (the new company 'perk' car) – partners in minor accountancy firms.
Isuzu Trooper: affluent Londoners with big families,
Jaguar: government ministers, magistrates, senior company executives whose firms insist on buying British.

Lada: bus drivers, car park attendants, Geordies.

Land Rover: (the ultimate fashion statement): *Defender* – rich farmers, expedition leaders; *Discovery* – advertising executives, Fleet Street photographers; *Range Rover* – film directors (if new), landed gentry (if older), self-employed builders (if clapped out).

Lexus: (a Mercedes clone): casino managers, self-made millionaires from the north.

Lotus: commercial photographers from the Midlands, super-models.

Maserati: sons of self-made millionaires.

Mazda, *sports cars only*: desperate bachelors for whom time is running out, car salesmen.

Mercedes-Benz: *C* – successful thirty-somethings; *E* and *S* – company secretaries, Harley Street doctors, senior public relations executives, all outside-lane roadhogs.

Mitsubishi: *Space Wagon* – environmental health officers; *Shogun* – advertising copywriters, interior designers.

Morgan: nostalgia freaks excited by the freedom of any 40 mph dual carriageway, wealthy Oxbridge students.

Nissan: *Micra* – middle-aged couples whose children have left home, nervous drivers; *300 ZX* – Premier Division footballers.

Peugeot: *205* – secretaries, typists; *405* – Liberal Democrat councillors, trading standards officers; *605* – university lecturers, vets.

Porsche: (the ageing yuppie status symbol): City dealers who started out in the 1980s, North Sea oil workers.

Proton: (a Ratner's car): Yorkshire miners, *Which?* readers.

Renault: *Clio* – young Sloanes; *19* – provincial yuppies; *21* – Asian businessmen; *Espace* – the 'other car' of the professional middle classes with families.

Rolls-Royce: Marbella drugs dealers, successful northern comedians.

Rover: (just a hint of wood on the dashboard to add respectability): *Mini* – au pairs, young television researchers; *Metro* – librarians; *Maestro* – priests, monks, nuns; *Montego* – funeral directors' 'other car'; *2-Series* – schoolteachers; *4-Series* – off-duty policemen; *8-series* – judges, MPs, officers in the armed forces, trade union leaders.

Saab: *900* – GPs, opticians; *9000* – hospital consultants.

Skoda: traffic wardens.

Vauxhall: (the purist's company car): *Astra* – junior salesmen; *Cavalier* – senior salesmen; *Calibra* – successful salesmen; *Carlton* – sales directors.

Volkswagen: *Beetle* – drop-outs, New Age fanatics; *Polo* – home helps, social workers; *Golf* – divorcees, yuppies still living in the 1980s.

Volvo: *440* – tax inspectors, local government officers, workaholics too busy to shop around; *850* – BMW drivers with dogs; *940, 960* – airline pilots, bank managers, headteachers.

CHAPTER TEN

THE UPS AND DOWNS OF CLASS

In Wigan the early-morning sound of the clumping of mill-girls' clogs is a distant echo from the town's working-class past. When George Orwell came down the road more than 50 years ago, he failed to find Wigan Pier – a music-hall joke, it seems – but found the evidence of poverty and oppression he was looking for. Ever since the Etonian's journey of discovery in the 1930s, the textile and mining town midway between Manchester and Liverpool has symbolised, either romantically or laughingly, the nostalgic stereotype of a cloth-capped, ragged-trousered proletariat suffering in the 'most class-ridden' of all societies. The power of the image has been immense, so much so that it has cloaked a changing reality. Even now, there is a litany of towns in the industrial north of England that conjure similar condescending, commercialised, politically exploited and intrinsically ahistoric caricatures: Barnsley, Scunthorpe, Salford, Widnes and Hartlepool, to name a few.

Wigan, birthplace of George Formby – whose father may have originated the Wigan Pier joke – and Joe Gormley, the former miners' leader, is a socially mobile town on the way up. The remnants of the imposing textile mills, bleak terraced streets and mired canal survive, but largely as reminders of a past that contrasts markedly with the present. If Orwell were to go today to Wigan – 'the filthy heart of civilisation' – in search of the traditional working class, he would have the same success that he had with the pier. It is a road to nowhere. The pits are closed and heavy industry is in terminal decline; the biggest employer, with a 2,000-strong workforce, is Heinz, makers of everything from baby food to baked beans at the biggest food manufacturing plant in Western Europe. In place of the traditional working class are the new members of a 'lumpen middle class', the erstwhile respectable working class but with sufficient disposable income or credit to finance a more bourgeois lifestyle. Not even Wigan has escaped the spread of middle-class values and habits. Indeed, like many working-class towns across the country, it has deliberately – if falteringly – pursued and promoted them.

The first sound in the mornings is the choking engines of the two-year-old Ford Escorts that clog the dual-carriageways into town-centre car parks. On one side is Central Park, the ground of Wigan Rugby Football Club, the Inter Milan or Real Madrid of the rugby world, with a team of expensive players that attract crowds of 18,000 or more; on the other are modern shopping malls clustered within a network of narrow, bustling streets. Incongruously twinned with Angers – 'set in the beautiful Loire valley of western France', according to Wigan's voluminous promotional literature – the town has embarked on a sustained programme of what can be best described as gentrification: turn-of-the-century textile mills have been converted and refurbished; the 'half-ruinous' houses where Orwell lodged in Wigan's Scholes area, home to Irish immigrants, have been demolished and replaced by neat maison-ettes and flats; one address he stayed at in Warrington Lane is now the site of the Sovereign Business Park, with local offices of Pearl Assurance and Southwestern Bell, the American telecommunications company. Further out, on the northern outskirts and ignored by Orwell, are the middle-class enclaves of Wigan Lane and Standish where solicitors, bank managers and middle-ranking executives of all kinds live.

In the heart of the town the old market hall has given way to the mock-Tudor façades of The Galleries, a £30 million shopping centre opened in the late 1980s and a red-brick monument to the consumer society. It could just as well be in Croydon, Woking or other prosperous centres across the southeast of England. Marks & Spencer, Debenhams, Boots, Asda, Kwik Save, the Co-op (Nor-mid) and Morrisons are all represented in the town; the only significant absentees are Sainsbury and Tesco (the latter closed its store in the late 1980s). In the indoor market you are as likely to find peppered steaks and garlic pâté as tripe or chitterlings. And in the autumnal rain of 1993 the windows of Thomas Cook were emblazoned with advertisements for Christmas shopping trips to New York – 'only £189 return' – and special offers to the

Caribbean. Many Wiganers were already booking summer holidays, with Majorca, Greece and Florida having long replaced Blackpool or Morecambe as the most popular destinations.

In *The Road to Wigan Pier*, Orwell wrote of the industrial north as 'a strange country' of unfamiliar scenery. 'There exists in England,' he said, 'a curious cult of Northernness, a sort of Northern snobbishness. A Yorkshireman in the South will always take care to let you know that he regards you as inferior. If you ask him why, he will explain that it is only in the North that life is "real", that the industrial work done in the North is the only "real" work, that the North is inhabited by "real" people, the South merely by rentiers and their parasites.' The shadow of a cultural identity hangs in the air, but the substance of its 'differentness' has disappeared: up to half the population of Wigan commutes to work in Bolton, Manchester or Liverpool; even in a property slump, the town can sustain nine estate agencies; of the 86 public houses that used to crowd the town centre, only 18 remain; body-building appears to have replaced beer as the local pastime, while the youth go to nightclubs with names such as JJ's or The Cowshed, indistinguishable from thousands of others that are venues for the 'rave culture' of the younger generation; and the only coal dust around is pure imitation, a sugary aniseed confection, packaged in 8oz jars and sold at £1.55 to tourists visiting the Wigan Pier museum that was created with the help of grants from the European Union. Like most Wiganers, John Winnard, joint managing director of the firm that produces the 'coal dust', is ambivalent about Orwell and his portrayal of the contemporary working class. 'We speak well of him, but he didn't do us any favours. He didn't present us in a good light. People expect us still to be in cloth caps,' says Winnard, whose company also sells mint balls to Selfridges and Harvey Nichols. 'Mind you, if that's what they want, that's what they get.'

How can a town like Wigan change so much? And what does it say about the 320,000 people who live there or in all the other traditional heartlands of the old working class? It is hardly a boom town, or a magnet for migrants from an alien middle class. It is, however, not only a microcosm of what has happened to the working class in general, but also the culmination of what has happened to millions of its members in particular. Towns like Wigan have changed their social composition simply because the individuals within them have changed their social class. The old working class has been deprived of its roots, its traditional work-places, its close-knit communities, its meeting places, its organisa-tions, and the uniform constraints on its lifestyles and opportunities. In return, it has acquired the wherewithal to take part in a society where the middle class gives the lead. The working class has been, quite literally, dismembered. And all of its disembodied parts are now free to become individuals in their own right, to sink or swim in a new social order.

The evidence is there in the remarkable decline in trade union membership, which is at its lowest since the Second World War. The proportion of the workforce who are members of TUC-affiliated unions has dropped below 30%, falling by 480,000 to 7.3 million in 1992. Significantly, some of the sharpest falls have been in the big industrial unions such as the Transport and General Workers' Union, a symptom of economic transition, unemploy-ment, and new social and political mores. The solidity of the working class has been dissolved and its component parts have been atomised: the workers now have not only their chains to lose, but also their homes, their mortgages and their cars. They have turned their backs on collectivism and embraced individualism; in 1979 the crucial electoral swing to Margaret Thatcher by the occupational C2s, the skilled manual working class, marked an end to hopes of mass social change and evinced widespread personal ambitions for individual social improvement. The result is a class reformation, in which people are grouped not by their occupational status – and hence, to a degree, by their geographical position: working-class north, middle-class south – but are brought together by similarities in their interests, lifestyles, cultural pastimes and habits. The interests they share are a source of class, while so-called 'class interests' are no longer a unifying bond. Members of the upwardly mobile working class, now in its second generation, are unlikely ever again to rediscover their old class identity.

The Royal Family has become one of the most downwardly mobile families of note. Moreover, no other has demonstrated so clearly how marriage can be the most efficient vehicle of upward mobility – and divorce the most rapid means of social descent. The fire at Windsor Castle towards the end of the 'annus horribilis' of 1992 revealed the gulf that has grown between royalty and a disillusioned populace that refuses unquestioning loyalty and de-ference to what increasingly appears like any ordinary middle-class family of taxpayers, with palaces. The Princess of Wales's transition from Sloane Ranger to 'fairy-tale princess' to pseudo-Essex Girl climaxed in even *Tatler* magazine reflecting snidely on her 'penchant for all things Chigwellian'. The antics of the younger royals and their failure to act as role-models or pursue serious careers have contrasted, confusingly, with the traditional aloofness of the Queen. Yet both are equally divorced from contemporary experience and only add to the popular sense of disenchantment. The royals are left bewildered, often amusing in their anachronistic naivety. 'In this country,' Prince Edward railed in *Majesty* magazine, 'we're always looking down, always looking in, trying to belittle ourselves. All this constant thing about class, for instance, which is the worst thing in the world Marx ever invented.' In a society that is ever more meritocratic, the royals have never done less to earn public respect and never failed so obviously to adapt to new circumstances. The more concessions they are forced to make to middle-class opinion, the more they appear like the many impoverished aristocratic families that have been forced reluctantly to open their stately homes to the paying public.

The monarchy clings on, however, to its central function of endorsing an obsolescent sense of hierarchy and being the source of patronage and honours. Despite John Major's much-heralded move towards 'classless' honours lists, the reality behind the hyperbole remains the same. If anything, the middle classes have tightened their grip on the old baubles of power. Newspaper headlines about honours – albeit minor ones – being awarded to taxi-drivers and traffic wardens disguise the truth that Major's so-called common touch has actually resulted in ordinary people getting an even smaller share of invitations to investitures at Buckingham Palace. In the 1994 New Year Honours List six in 10 awards went to members of the traditional middle-class élite of senior civil servants, politicians and wealthy businessmen. The proportion of 'gongs' going to the working class dropped to less than a quarter; fewer than one in 25 went to those in unskilled manual jobs done by nearly half the nation's workforce. Even when it came to the MBE, the least class-ridden honour under the 'new' system, four in 10 went to people in the top two occupational groups. Tinkering with the honours system is designed to buy continued loyalty of the masses to an outdated system of inherited privilege, social hierarchy and political favouritism. One Labour

MP condemned it as window-dressing: 'The highest awards still go to backbench Tory MPs with 20 years' loyal service, and the lowest go to the local voluntary or community worker. Perhaps we might believe there has been a reform of the honours system when the Tory MP gets the MBE and the community worker gets the knighthood.' If Major were serious about creating a 'classless' society that has any substance beyond easy newspaper headlines, a symbolic starting point would be the abolition of the honours system.

The new élite, though, are unmoved by the prospect of peerages, knighthoods or other lesser awards in the debased currency of the honours system. Their status depends on the substance of their achievements. They not only epitomise a transformation of society, they are also active agents and propagators of change within it. In essence, they are evangelists of the egalitarian capitalism that has enabled more and more people to share in the lifestyles that were once the preserve of the old narrow middle class and the even narrower upper class. They are often opinion-formers in the media or in the business of wealth creation, and are less frequently found in the traditional professions than in entrepreneurial service industries, computing and high technology. They are notable for being cosmopolitan rather than 'Little Englanders', ambitious and driven rather than complacent or complaisant. They create a demand and satisfy it rather than simply respond to developments in which they have no part. They are demotic in their outlook, addressing society as a whole rather than catering for any particular groups within it. Their original social background is largely irrelevant, but – unlike many conditioned by a 'liberal' education – they see no shame in proclaiming they are middle class. Indeed, they are proud of it.

Class is now less a measure of what makes you similar to others in a group; it is a mark of what distinguishes you from other individuals – the process of 'ruling out' others that, ironically, Evelyn Waugh wrote about so superciliously. It is a definition of difference, and never before have there been so many opportunities to assert that difference. In particular, the importance of knowledge – what you know as much as what you do – has become central: a knowledge of fine wines can elevate you, as can a knowledge of what is in the quality broadsheet newspapers rather than what are the headlines in the tabloids, or a knowledge of the plays, films and books of the moment. That is why the three-dimensional, holistic approach is central to the production of a ready-reckoner of class that can tell you where you are, at any given time, in the pecking order. It can provide a constant reference point in ever-changing circumstances. It is true that even under traditional methods of social classifications it is possible for people to change their class: strangely, however, the only way they can apparently do this is by changing their occupation. For example, the daughter of a miner who becomes a sales executive is officially deemed to have moved up the class ladder. According to orthodox approaches to class, however, there was no change when she became the first in her family to attend grammar school, to get academic qualifications, to go to university, to buy her own house, or to become an opera buff; it suddenly happened, we are told, when she got a new job. Everything else is regarded as contributing to her eventual upward mobility rather than evidence of a gradual ascendancy. Such an approach is clearly wrong-headed: it assumes that all the people in the same job are of the same class. Yet all you have to do to prove the assumption wrong is look around your office at people whose career position is on a par with yours. Is it only the broad similarities that strike you, or the individual differences as well?

'The New Poor of yesteryear are fighting a losing battle. To remain poor needs the utmost skill and ingenuity,' observed George Mikes, the writer. There is, of course, an entrenched minority of people stuck at the bottom of the pile. Appropriately called the underclass, they are *beneath* class: generally unemployed, often single parents or living in dislocated families, and so divorced from the rest of society that crime is a seductive way of life. Unlike the old working class, they have been left behind and have failed to cross the threshold of material well-being that allows a foothold on the social ladder. Once on the ladder, it is possible – even without changing your occupation – to change your class. It is a process of recreation, of swimming with the tide of social change, of participating in the prevailing lifestyles of those regarded as having higher status. It is not, however, simply specious imitation; it is a constant refusal to 'know your place' and a constant awareness of how to improve your position by making the most of the many opportunities to do so. Ultimately, it is learning what your house, your car, your possessions, habits and aspirations intrinsically say about you, and acting on the knowledge if you wish them to say something different.

The chattering classes and London-based social commentators, who were appalled by the Yuppiedom of the late 1980s – a phenomenon they helped create by defining it – have been quick to report its alleged demise. In fact, its influence has been popularised, seeping downwards, socially, and spreading across the country, geographically. In far-flung corners of the kingdom, it is possible to see the aspiring heirs to their high-earning, high-achieving ways both at work and at play. It is fashionable in some circles in the 1990s to sneer at self-improvement, even though those who sneer are often those who have themselves improved their status. Having climbed the ladder, there are some who then want to pull it up after them. The hegemony of the new middle class has left their superannuated predecessors in limbo: prosperous and secure in their traditional careers and lifestyles – but debilitated by a 'liberal' education that has filled them with angst about their relative good fortune. They do not share the dynamism of the upwardly mobile; their offspring and heirs often lack the drive to achieve a social momentum, and so are at risk of being overtaken in the new pecking order.

Sometimes it is an advantage if your past 'catches up' with you; sometimes it is a disadvantage. As young adults, the offspring of middle-class parents can plunge down the social order, merely treading water in a fairly ordinary career and maintaining a decent lifestyle only because it is buttressed by liberal infusions of parental cash. However, the same people in their 30s or 40s can suddenly find themselves inheriting their parents' home and money – or those of other close relatives. Immediately, their class is jolted back up the ladder. Conversely, the offspring of working-class parents can surge upwards in their 20s or 30s only to receive a setback in their job or marriage – divorce can be a shocking downwardly mobile experience – and they find they have lost all they had previously gained, without the safety net of having a middle-class family or middle-class inheritance to fall back on. For everybody, there are crucial times when a wrong choice – or dilatoriness in making the most of an opportunity – can be damaging: the decision to leave school at 16, not go to university, or failure to exploit a moment of good fortune in your career. *Carpe diem* (seize the day) is a good motto for all aspiring class warriors, the most successful of whom seize every moment that comes along.

The last decade of the 20th century marks the dominance of the new middle-class 'settlement' following the Thatcher revolution, the ramifications of which are still developing. It is no coincidence that John Major and George Carey, heads of government and church, have risen from humble beginnings to the apex of society. The future is one in which the social environment will be even more open, and much more amenable to the upwardly mobile. Only the self-defining failures, those who accept obsolete exhortations to know their place, will exclude themselves from the process of individualised social progress. If there is one distinguishing trait of the new middle class, it is confidence in the future and the belief that it can be better than the present – culturally, materially and meritocratically. Pessimism and short-termism are hallmarks of the old working class or the desperately downwardly mobile. The three-dimensional view recognises the fluidity and complexity of class. It is not just about the here and now, or the past and the legacy it bestows. It is not just about the job you do, or the money you have, or the home you own, or the car you drive, or the lifestyle you follow. It is all these things, the sum that is greater than all its parts.

In future, it will be possible for people to pay as much attention to improving their class as they do now to maintaining their health. Class will be a means of liberation rather than incarceration. By wisely exercising choice – and we have seen how class is essentially a matter of choice for millions more people – you open up the opportunity of more choice, and more self-improvement. Class creates order out of chaos, and gives meaningful direction to the lives of individuals. In a society in which middle-class values predominate, class is not as deeply or destructively divisive as once it was. Indeed, the shared values and ambitions implied by a commonly accepted class structure provide society with coherence and stability. A 'classless society' would be uncivilised anarchy: a society without class would not be a society at all.

HOW YOU SCORE ON QUESTIONS OF CLASS

The scoresheet is divided into three sections – past, present and future – enabling you ultimately to discover whether you are on the way up, on the way down or stagnating. You can also find out your overall score by adding together the totals for each of the three sections. In the questionnaire there were 11 questions relating to your past, 39 concerning your present, and 10 assessing your future aspirations.

Scoring your past

8. Inheritance – The most important class indicator of your past, and one that can spur you on the road to upward mobility.
   a) 50; **b)** 45; **c)** 40; **d)** 35; **e)** 20; **f)** 10; **g)** 0.

11. Parental occupations – They are less important than your own job, but are, nevertheless, a weighty part of the 'baggage' you carry later in life.
   a) 35; **b)** 30; **c)** 20; **d)** 15; **e)** 5; **f)** 0.

14. Primary education – It provides the first social environment outside the family home, although it is less relevant than secondary schooling.
   a) 25; **b)** 5; **c)** 15.

15. Secondary education – A wide variety of choice makes the type of school you went to particularly important.
   a) 30; **b)** 40; **c)** 10; **d)** 20; **e)** 5; **f)** 30.

16. Leaving school – Premature departure can make later progress an uphill struggle and cause much regret.
   a) –10; **b)** 0 **c)** 10.

17. Higher education – It provides a multitude of options that produce the ultimate educational pecking order. Higher education is the great social sifter.
   a) 18; **b)** 15; **c)** 15; **d)** 8; **e)** 8; **f)** 20; **g)** 18; **h)** 10; **i)** 10; **j)** 10;
   k) 20; **l)** 10; **m)** 10; **n)** 18; **o)** 15; **p)** 15; **q)** 15; **r)** 15; **s)** 18; **t)** 15;
   u) 18; **v)** 15; **w)** 15; **x)** 10; **y)** 10; **z)** 0.

18. Degree – With more people than ever going on to higher education, it is a severe disadvantage not to have a degree.
   a) 25; **b)** 0.

19. Father's education – It is less important than your own education, but nevertheless a social signifier that indicates how well established your class position is.
   a) 15; **b)** 5; **c)** 10.

APPENDIX I

20. Mother's education.

   a) 15; **b)** 5; **c)** 10.

21. Parents' higher education – Like your parents' schooling, it provides evidence of your class origins.

   a) 15; **b)** 10; **c)** 0.

60. Class counterfeiting – Everyone indulges in a little social climbing, but outright lies and deception suggest insecurity and misunderstanding about your class position.

   a) –3; **b)** –2; **c)** –1; **d)** –3; **e)** –1; **f)** –2; **g)** –2; **h)** 5.

Total score for your past: _____

Scoring your present

1. Earnings – What you are paid is a cornerstone of your class.
   a) 50; **b)** 40; **c)** 35; **d)** 30; **e)** 20; **f)** 15; **g)** 10; **h)** 0.

3. Perks – The benefits in kind derived from your occupation can be substantial and can be either the icing on the cake or compensation for a more modest salary.
   a) 3; **b)** 5; **c)** 5; **d)** 2; **e)** 2; **f)** 3; **g)** 2; **h)** 3; **i)** 3; **j)** 5; **k)** 5; **l)** 2; **m)** 0.

4. Bank account – The name of the bank on your cheque book can be an emblem of your status.
   a) 5; **b)** 3; **c)** 3; **d)** 3; **e)** 5; **f)** 10; **g)** 3; **h)** 3; **i)** 10; **j)** 5; **k)** 3; **l)** 10; **m)** 7; **n)** 3; **o)** 3; **p)** 7; **q)** 3; **r)** 3; **s)** 5; **t)** 3; **u)** 5; **v)** 0.

5. Savings – The amount of money you save is evidence of how comfortably off you are after paying your routine bills.
   a) 40; **b)** 35; **c)** 30; **d)** 25; **e)** 15; **f)** 10; **g)** 0.

6. Credit cards – Your credit rating is an independent assessment indicating how much others think you are worth.
   a) 40; **b)** 35; **c)** 30; **d)** 25; **e)** 15; **f)** 10; **g)** 0.

7. Stocks and shares – Investments are a measure of your stake in society and your confidence in the future.
   a) 40; **b)** 35; **c)** 30; **d)** 25; **e)** 15; **f)** 10; **g)** 0.

10. Occupation – The job you do is another cornerstone of your class that merits high marks.
   a) 50; **b)** 40; **c)** 30; **d)** 20; **e)** 10; **f)** 0.

12. Wealth – To be less well-off than your parents is a sign of impending downward mobility.
   a) 10; **b)** 5; **c)** 0; **d)** –5; **e)** –10.

22. Type of home – The property you inhabit is a more than a roof over your head. The variety of homes produces an elaborate hierarchy.
   a) 0; **b)** 20; **c)** 25; **d)** 25; **e)** 20; **f)** 10; **g)** 30; **h)** 25; **i)** 15; **j)** 10.

23. Age of home – Some period properties are more desirable than others.
   a) 18; **b)** 20; **c)** 15; **d)** 15; **e)** 12; **f)** 10; **g)** 10; **h)** 10.

24. Home-ownership – Owning your own home is as important as your salary or your job in defining your class position.

  a) 50; **b)** 0; **c)** 5; **d)** 25.

25. House price – The value of your home, or the size of your mortgage, embodies your financial status and epitomises your social standing. It is another cornerstone of class.

  a) 50; **b)** 45; **c)** 40; **d)** 35; **e)** 30; **f)** 25; **g)** 20; **h)** 15; **i)** 10; **j)** 0.

26. Number of bedrooms – The size of your home is important.

  a) 15; **b)** 13; **c)** 10; **d)** 5; **e)** 1; **f)** 0.

27. Number of bathrooms – How many bathrooms you have can be a source of one-upmanship.

  a) 15; **b)** 13; **c)** 5; **d)** 0.

28. Size of garden – An expanse of garden can be the crowning glory that adds status to your home.

  a) 15; **b)** 13; **c)** 10; **d)** 10; **e)** 8; **f)** 5; **g)** 2; **h)** 2; **i)** 1; **j)** 1; **k)** 0.

29. Cars – Owning one car is no longer out of the ordinary. It takes two or three to make you stand out.

  a) 15; **b)** 10; **c)** 5; **d)** 0.

30. Value of car – A car is a status symbol that you can take anywhere. Although price is important, it cannot quite compare with the value of your home.

  a) 40; **b)** 35; **c)** 30; **d)** 20; **e)** 15; **f)** 5; **g)** 1; **h)** 0.

31. Possessions – A full portfolio of possessions reflects taste as well as wealth, and each one is a benchmark of class.

  a) 2; **b)** 2; **c)** 2; **d)** 1; **e)** 2; **f)** 2; **g)** 3; **h)** 5; **i)** 4; **j)** 4; **k)** 2; **l)** 5; **m)** 5; **n)** 2; **o)** 5; **p)** 1; **q)** 4; **r)** 3; **s)** 5; **t)** 4; **u)** 5; **v)** 5; **w)** 2; **x)** 1; **y)** 5; **z)** −10.

32. Services – You can score well by employing others to do the jobs that the upwardly mobile find a chore.

  a) 7; **b)** 10; **c)** 10; **d)** 5; **e)** 7; **f)** 10; **g)** 5; **h)** 10; **i)** 5; **j)** 7; **k)** 5; **l)** 0.

33. Daily newspapers – Editors target specific groups of readers. In a diverse market, your favourite newspaper mirrors your class attitudes and tastes.

  a) 0; **b)** 7; **c)** 0; **d)** 0; **e)** 0; **f)** 7 **g)** 10; **h)** 7; **i)** 7; **j)** 7; **k)** 10; **l)** 10; **m)** 5; **n)** 10; **o)** 5; **p)** 7; **q)** 10; **r)** 5; **s)** 7; **t)** 3; **u)** 10; **v)** −5.

34. Sunday newspapers – As above.

a) 10; **b)** 7; **c)** 0; **d)** 7; **e)** 0; **f)** 7; **g)** 5; **h)** 7; **i)** 0; **j)** 0; **k)** 7; **l)** 10; **m)** 7; **n)** –5.

35. Television – Like newspapers, every channel caters for a different audience.

a) 7; **b)** 10; **c)** 10; **d)** 5; **e)** 5; **f)** 0; **g)** 7; **h)** 5; **i)** 7; **j)** 5; **k)** 5.

36. Radio – As above.

a) 5; **b)** 7; **c)** 10; **d)** 10; **e)** 5; **f)** 7; **g)** 7; **h)** 5; **i)** 7; **j)** 5; **k)** 5.

37. Food shopping – Class-conscious consumers choose their supermarkets not just because of their convenience, but also because of their cachet.

a) 5; **b)** 5; **c)** 10; **d)** 10; **e)** 15; **f)** 2; **g)** 1; **h)** 15; **i)** 2; **j)** 2; **k)** 3; **l)** 13; **m)** 5; **n)** 10; **o)** 13; **p)** 2; **q)** 5; **r)** 13; **s)** 5; **t)** 2.

38. Clothes shopping – Shoppers do not choose stores simply according to the prices they charge. Every store has a different social profile.

a) 2; **b)** 2; **c)** 2; **d)** 5; **e)** 2; **f)** 0; **g)** 7; **h)** 0; **i)** 7; **j)** 10; **k)** 5; **l)** 7; **m)** 7; **n)** 5; **o)** 5; **p)** 10; **q)** 2; **r)** 5; **s)** 2; **t)** 5; **u)** 0; **v)** 7; **w)** 7; **x)** 5; **y)** 0; **z)** 0.

41. Leisure pursuits – There are bonuses to be had for those who have the time and money to enjoy an array of pastimes.

a) 3; **b)** 0; **c)** 2; **d)** 2; **e)** 2; **f)** 3; **g)** 0; **h)** 1; **i)** 3; **j)** 3; **k)** 0; **l)** 3; **m)** 3; **n)** 3; **o)** 1; **p)** 2; **q)** 3; **r)** 2; **s)** 3; **t)** 3; **u)** 1; **v)** 1; **w)** 2; **x)** 3; **y)** 2; **z)** 0.

43. Drinks – What you drink provides one of the sharpest tests of taste.

a) 1; **b)** 1; **c)** 2; **d)** 3; **e)** 4; **f)** 5; **g)** 5; **h)** 4; **i)** 4; **j)** 3; **k)** 4; **l)** 2; **m)** 0; **n)** 1; **o)** 0; **p)** 0; **q)** 3; **r)** 2; **s)** 5; **t)** 0; **u)** 3; **v)** 2; **w)** 5; **x)** 2; **y)** 1; **z)** 0.

44. Dining out – Because dining out has become commonplace, the amount you are prepared to pay is the distinguishing mark.

a) 15; **b)** 13; **c)** 10; **d)** 7; **e)** 7; **f)** 7; **g)** 5; **h)** 5; **i)** 3; **j)** 0; **k)** 0.

46. Male film stars – The celebrities you admire can personify your class ideal.

a) 2; **b)** 3; **c)** 1; **d)** 2; **e)** 1; **f)** 3; **g)** 3; **h)** 3; **i)** 1; **j)** 2; **k)** 2; **l)** 2; **m)** 1; **n)** 1; **o)** 2; **p)** 1; **q)** 5.

47. Female film stars – As above.
   a) 2; **b)** 2; **c)** 0; **d)** 2; **e)** 1; **f)** 2; **g)** 2; **h)** 1; **i)** 3; **j)** 2; **k)** 2; **l)** 1;
   m) 3; **n)** 1; **o)** 2; **p)** 2; **q)** 5.

48. Authors – As above.
   a) 2; **b)** 3; **c)** 3; **d)** 1; **e)** 1; **f)** 1; **g)** 1; **h)** 2; **i)** 2; **j)** 2; **k)** 1; **l)** 1;
   m) 2; **n)** 2; **o)** 1; **p)** 1; **q)** 3; **r)** 2; **s)** 2; **t)** 2; **u)** 3.

49. Reading – In a technological age, the art of reading is a minority
pastime beloved of the middle classes.
   a) 4; **b)** 1; **c)** 5; **d)** 2; **e)** 3; **f)** 0.

50. Male public figures – By their nature, true class warriors are
judicious in their choice of heroes.
   a) 1; **b)** 0; **c)** 0 **d)** 2; **e)** 0; **f)** 2; **g)** 1; **h)** 0; **i)** 2; **j)** 3; **k)** 3 **l)** 3; **m)** 2;
   n) 3; **o)** 0; **p)** 1; **q)** 5.

51. Female public figures – As above.
   a) 2 **b)** 2; **c)** 1 **d)** 2; **e)** 2; **f)** 2; **g)** 2; **h)** 2; **i)** 3; **j)** 1; **k)** 1; **l)** 2; **m)** 3;
   n) 3; **o)** 0; **p)** 2; **q)** 5.

55. Vocabulary: The words you use can betray a lot about you.
   a) 2; **b)** 0; **c)** 5; **d)** 3; **e)** 1; **f)** 1; **g)** 3; **h)** 2; **i)** 0.

56.
   a) 0; **b)** 0; **c)** 5; **d)** 0.

57.
   a) 0; **b)** 3; **c)** 5; **d)** 0; **e)** 0.

58.
   a) 5; **b)** 3; **c)** 5; **d)** 0; **e)** 0.

59.
   a) 0; **b)** 5; **c)** 0; **d)** 4; **e)** 2; **f)** 3; **g)** 0.

Total score for your present circumstances: _____

Scoring your future

2. Future earnings – The increase you expect in your salary is a measure of your class security and your confidence in the future. Only those on the way down believe their earnings will decrease.
 a) 35; **b)** 30; **c)** 20; **d)** 15; **e)** 10; **f)** 0; **g)** –10.

9. Inheritance – The prospect of a windfall allows you to be more adventurous, enabling you to pursue ambitious goals.
 a) 25; **b)** 20; **c)** 15; **d)** 10; **e)** 5; **f)** 3; **g)** 0.

13. Wealth – The salary you think you will need before you will feel wealthy is one of the most significant benchmarks of your attitude to material prosperity.
 a) 40; **b)** 35; **c)** 30; **d)** 25; **e)** 15; **f)** 10; **g)** 5; **h)** 1.

39. Men's clothing – You can lose marks as well as gain them by the sort of clothes you aspire to wear.
 a) 7; **b)** 7; **c)** 0; **d)** 4; **e)** 7; **f)** 0; **g)** 8; **h)** 0; **i)** 2; **j)** –5; **k)** 5; **l)** 4; **m)** –5; **n)** 8; **o)** 5; **p)** 0.

40. Women's clothing – As above.
 a) 7; **b)** 4; **c)** 0; **d)** 7; **e)** 8; **f)** 4; **g)** 5; **h)** – 5; **i)** 7; **j)** 5; **k)** – 5; **l)** 2; **m)** –5; **n)** –5; **o)** 4; **p)** 0.

42. Social calendar – Who you want to rub shoulders with is an indicator of your class aspirations.
 a) 7; **b)** 7; **c)** 5; **d)** 2; **e)** 4; **f)** 4; **g)** 3; **h)** 7; **i)** 3; **j)** 1; **k)** 7; **l)** 7; **m)** 3; **n)** 7; **o)** 7; **p)** 5; **q)** 5; **r)** 7; **s)** 2; **t)** 4; **u)** 3; **v)** 3; **w)** 2; **x)** 1; **y)** 0; **z)** 0.

45. Holidays – With so many people taking regular foreign holidays, the choice of destination is crucial.
 a) 10; **b)** 12; **c)** 1; **d)** 1; **e)** 15; **f)** 15; **g)** 2; **h)** 7; **i)** 5; **j)** 5; **k)** 15; **l)** 12; **m)** 12; **n)** 12; **o)** 7; **p)** 12; **q)** 7; **r)** 7; **s)** 12; **t)** 0.

52. Boys' names – What you call your children often encapsulates the sort of future you want for them. The names parents choose are frequently ones associated with families in a slightly higher social class.
 a) 5; **b)** 10; **c)** 3; **d)** 7; **e)** 5; **f)** 1; **g)** 5; **h)** 0; **i)** 0; **j)** 10; **k)** 10; **l)** 10; **m)** 10; **n)** 0; **o)** 0; **p)** 0; **q)** 5; **r)** 1; **s)** 5; **t)** 10; **u)** 10; **v)** 7; **w)** 0; **x)** 7; **y)** 10; **z)** 10.

53. Girls' names – As above.

   a) 7; **b)** 10; **c)** 5; **d)** 7; **e)** 10; **f)** 3; **g)** 10; **h)** 10; **i)** 7; **j)** 10; **k)** 3;
   l) 10; **m)** 7; **n)** 7; **o)** 7; **p)** 7; **q)** 1; **r)** 0; **s)** 10; **t)** 10; **u)** 5; **v)** 5;
   w) 7; **x)** 0; **y)** 10; **z)** 0.

54. Children's activities – The activities that parents choose for their children increasingly articulate their own interests and ambitions. The wrong choice can reflect badly on their own class potential.

   a) 3; **b)** 0; **c)** 1; **d)** 2; **e)** 0; **f)** 3; **g)** 3; **h)** 1; **i)** 0; **j)** 3; **k)** 2; **l)** 1;
   m) 3; **n)** 3; **o)** 2; **p)** 1; **q)** 0; **r)** 2; **s)** 0.

Total score for your future: ————

THE THREE-DIMENSIONAL VIEW OF CLASS

Are you a triple-A or a triple-Z? The three-dimensional view of class takes account of your past, present and future, uniquely reflecting the dynamism of your social mobility. Your class position can easily be expressed in a series of three letters of the alphabet. The first letter refers to your past and, if you had the best possible start in life, you could well be an A here. The second letter refers to your present and, if you are currently making a success of your life, you could be an A here, too. The third letter refers to your future and, if your prospects and aspirations could not be higher, you could qualify for your third A in a row. At the other end of the spectrum from the AAAs are those trapped at the bottom of the pile: no past to speak of, no present to be proud of, and little hope for the future. They are the ZZZs.

To find out which you are, take the three scores for your past, present, and future and see where they put you on the following scales:

Past

A 260 or more; **B** 250–259; **C** 240–249; **D** 230–239; **E** 220–229; **F** 210–219; **G** 200–209; **H** 190–199; **I** 180–189; **J** 170–179; **K** 160–169; **L** 150–159; **M** 140–149; **N** 130–139; **O** 120–129; **P** 110–119; **Q** 100–109; **R** 90–99; **S** 80–89; **T** 70–79; **U** 60–69; **V** 50–59; **W** 40–49; **X** 30–39; **Y** 20–29; **Z** 19 or less.

Present

A 770 or more; **B** 740–769; **C** 710–739; **D** 680–709; **E** 650–679; **F** 620–649; **G** 590–619; **H** 560–589; **I** 530–559; **J** 500–529; **K** 470–499; **L** 440–469; **M** 410–439; **N** 380–409; **O** 350–379; **P** 320–349; **Q** 290–319; **R** 260–289; **S** 230–259; **T** 200–229; **U** 170–199; **V** 140–169; **W** 110–139; **X** 80–109; **Y** 50–79; **Z** 49 or less.

Future

A 125 or more; **B** 120–124; **C** 115–119; **D** 110–114; **E** 105–109; **F** 100–104; **G** 95–99; **H** 90–94; **I** 85–89; **J** 80–84; **K** 75–79; **L** 70–74; **M** 65–69; **N** 60–64; **O** 55–59; **P** 50–54; **Q** 45–49; **R** 40–44; **S** 35–39; **T** 30–34; **U** 25–29; **V** 20–24; **W** 15–19; **X** 10–14; **Y** 5–9; **Z** 4 or less.

A NEW SOCIAL MAP FOR BRITAIN:
THE A–Z OF CLASS

So are you part of the new middle class, and where do you fit in? The extra dimensions of the A–Z of class go beyond a mere snapshot of where you happen to be right now on the social ladder. They tell you whether you are a class migrant on the way up or on the way down, or socially static.

If your first letter – the one determined by your past – comes earlier in the alphabet than the second letter, you are failing to live up to the standard set by your background and are not making the most of the advantages it provided. Conversely, if it comes later in the alphabet, then you have escaped or, at least, improved on your background by climbing the ladder.

However, it is the second letter in your triple-letter grade – the one determined by present circumstances – that is key. If it is A, B or C, you are clearly ranked among the new élite or are a member of the old aristocracy who has successfully survived meritocratic change. If it is X, Y or Z, you are firmly anchored in the underclass. In between is the crowded middle ground, occupied by millions of individuals, that conventional social classifications have proved incapable of stratifying. In the very middle of the new social alphabet are those whose middle letter is an M. They embody middle-class lifestyles, even though many of them may have come from working-class backgrounds and still see themselves as 'true to their roots'.

Your third letter – the one determined by your prospects and aspirations – is a measure of what you expect the future to hold and your attitude to the choices it may offer. It can confirm the direction in which your class position is heading: it can either reinforce your upward mobility or downward mobility. It can also indicate that your class decline may yet be reversed, or it can suggest that you are at your peak. For example, if the third letter is the nearest of the three to the end of the alphabet, your lack of ambition means you risk losing the status you have already achieved.

For some people the triple-letter grade will show that their class position lacks dynamism. If all the letters are the same, it means you are no further on than where you started from, and are content for it to stay that way. Of course, that is all very well for the triple-As and, maybe, even for the triple-Ms. But for the triple-Ps? And the triple-Ts? In a perpetual game of snakes and ladders, today's socially static can quickly become tomorrow's downwardly mobile. Even the most successful class warrior cannot afford to be complacent. You need to monitor your class position at every turn: when you change job, when you move house, when you buy a new car, even when deciding which clothes you should wear.

For too long we have all been pigeon-holed to serve the needs of others. For their own ends, market researchers and advertisers have built lucrative careers out of crude over-simplifications intended to exploit mass markets. To them, the three-dimensional view of class is meaningless: they are not in the business of establishing whether or not we are keeping up with the Joneses. The ultimate class ladder is clearly impracticable: it would have as many rungs as there are people. However, it is no use to us to be herded into a small number of obsolete social groups; what we want to know is where we stand in relation to other individuals. A three-dimensional approach provides the answer.

GROUP A

Partner in firm of chartered accountants
Actor at top of profession
Admiral
Air Marshal
Ambassador
Medical consultant
Partner in firm of architects
Auditor of Court in Scotland
Bank manager of large branch
Barrister
Bishop
Captain of large merchant ship
Airline captain
Chief constable
Senior engineer
Chief executive or town clerk in local government
Company director of firm with 200-plus employees
Conductor of national orchestra
Coroner
Creative director in large advertising agency
Editor of national newspaper
Partner in estate agency
Large landholding farmer
Field Marshal
General practitioner or dental surgeon with own practice
Headteacher in large secondary school

Senior Inland Revenue inspector
Insurance underwriter
Principal Stock Exchange jobber
Judge
Management services manager in computers
Member of Parliament
Painter or artist at top of profession
Permanent Secretary in civil service
Power station manager
University professor
Senior hospital administrator
Sheriff in Scottish courts
Partner in firm of solicitors
Partner in firm of stockbrokers
Veterinary surgeon

GROUP B

West End actor
Air traffic controller
Archdeacon
Architect
Diplomatic attaché
Auctioneer
Qualified brewer
National radio broadcaster
School chaplain
Charge nurse
Chef with more than 25 staff
Computer programmer
Company director with 25 to 200 employees
Conductor of provincial orchestra
Stock Exchange dealer
Police inspector
Provincial newspaper editor
Estate agent
Executive officer in civil service
Farmer with small landholding
Film editor
Financial analyst
Headteacher in primary school
Tax inspector
National television interviewer
National newspaper correspondent
Senior laboratory technician
University lecturer
Commercial loss adjuster
Army major
Leader or soloist with provincial orchestra
Operations engineer in nuclear power station
Parish priest
Pilot
Public relations officer
Principal local government officer
Prison governor
Psychiatrist

Rabbi
Nursing sister
Social worker
RAF squadron leader
Stockbroker
Secondary schoolteacher
College lecturer
Television director

GROUP C

Accounts clerk
Acrobat
Assistant teacher
Athlete
Bailiff
Bank clerk
Boatswain (Bo'sun)
Bookmaker
Boxer
Local radio broadcaster
Bus inspector
Television camera operator
Car sales representative
Dispensing chemist
Naval chief petty officer
Chorus girl/boy
Community worker
Company director with fewer than 25 employees
Computer operator
Police constable
Local newspaper correspondent
Curate
Decorator
Dental hygienist
Dietician
Driving instructor
Fashion model
Filing clerk
Film extra
Leading firefighter
Footballer
Insurance sales representative
Disc jockey
Racing jockey
Laboratory technician
Qualified masseur/masseuse
Midwife
Qualified nanny

Nun
Nurse
Office worker
Optician
Pawnbroker
RSPCA inspector
Secretary
Army sergeant
Student
Travelling salesperson

GROUP D

AA or RAC patrol officer
Able seaman
Air steward/stewardess
Ambulance officer
Antique dealer
Skilled baker
Barber
Bar manager
Qualified beautician
Blacksmith
Boatbuilder
Bookbinder
Boot and shoe maker
Bricklayer
Builder and decorator
Bus driver
Butcher
Butler
Cabinet maker
Caretaker
Carpenter and joiner
Caterer
Chimney sweep
Cobbler
Commissionaire in Corps of Commissionaires
Compositor
Cooper
Coppersmith
Army corporal
Head cowherd
Coxswain
Crane and hoist operator
Cutter in bespoke tailoring
Dairy worker
Deep-sea diver
Skilled demolition worker
Dental technician
Docker

Dog handler
Drayman
Dressmaker
Electrician
Hand embroiderer
Train driver
Engraver
Explosives worker
Ordinary fire fighter
Fitter
Florist
Forester
Foundry worker
Furrier
Garage mechanic
Gardener
Gas engineer
Glazier
Goldsmith
Railway guard
Gunsmith
Hairdresser
Head waiter/waitress
Ironworker
Jeweller
Launderette manager
Lighthouse keeper
Locksmith
London taxi driver
Lorry driver
Market stallholder with employees
Mason
Milliner
Skilled miner
Mortician
Musical instrument maker
Panel beater
Piano tuner
Plasterer
Plumber

Head porter
Postal worker
Printer
Prison officer
Riveter
Shop assistant
Scaffolder
Merchant seaman
Skilled sewage worker
Signwriter
Slaughterhouse worker
Steeplejack
Stevedore
Bespoke tailor
Hospital theatre technician
Toolmaker
Watchmaker and repairer
Welder

GROUP E

Ordinary seaman
Army private
Bodyguard
Police cadet
Auxiliary nurse
Church warden
School crossing patroller
School caretaker
Au pair
Bar staff
Bingo caller
Binman
Holiday camp worker
Building labourer
Bus conductor
Caddie
Car park attendant
Chauffeur
Cleaner
Hotel cleaner
Supermarket checkout operator
Child minder
Coalman
Despatch courier
Croupier
School-dinner supervisor
Minicab driver
Dry cleaner
Petrol forecourt attendant
Forklift truck driver
Furnace operator
Handyman/woman
Hotel porter
Labourer
Market stallholder without employees
Market trader
Milk deliverer
Night security officer

Park keeper
Rag & bone collector
Railway porter
Rent collector
Roadsweeper
Servant
Traffic warden
Van driver
Waitress/waiter
Window cleaner

GROUP F

People entirely dependent on long-term state benefits – including those out of work for more than six months – because of sickness, unemployment, old age or other reasons.

Widows who receive only widows' benefit.

Casual or seasonal workers and those without regular income.

BIBLIOGRAPHY

Acorn User Guide, The (CACI Information Services, 1993)

Advertising Association, The, *Lifestyle Pocket Book* (NTC Publications, 1993)

– *Marketing Pocket Book* (NTC Publications, 1994)

Argyle, Michael, *The Psychology of Social Class* (Routledge, 1994)

Arthur Anderson Corporate Register, The (Hemmington Scott, 1993)

Barthes, Roland, *Mythologies* (Jonathan Cape, 1957)

Barr, Ann and York, Peter, *The Official Sloane Ranger Handbook* (Harpers and Queen, 1982)

Beresford, Richard with Boyd, Stephen, *The Sunday Times: Britain's Rich – The Top 400* (Times Newspapers, 1993)

– *The Sunday Times: Britain's Richest 500* (Times Newspapers, 1994)

Berthoud, Richard and Kempson, Elaine, *Credit and Debt in Britain* (Policy Studies Institute, 1990)

British Lifestyles (Mintel, 1994)

Cannadine, David, *The Decline and Fall of the British Aristocracy* (Pan, 1990)

Cathelat, Bernard, *Socio-Styles* (Kogan Page, 1990)

Central Statistical Office, *Family Spending* (HMSO, 1993)

– Regional Trends 28 (HMSO, 1993)

– Social Trends 24 (HMSO, 1994)

Chignell, Hugh, *Data in Sociology* (Causeway Press, 1990)

Cooper, Jilly, *Class* (Eyre Methuen, 1979)

Credit Card Research Group, *Card Expenditure Statistics* (HMSO, 1993)

– *Giving Credit Where Credit is Due, 1993 Britain* (HMSO 1994)

Cultural Trends (Policy Studies Institute, 1993)

Department of Employment, *New Earnings Survey* (HMSO, 1993)

Devlin, Tim and Williams, Hywel, *Old School Ties* (Sinclair-Stevenson, 1992)

Dunkling, Leslie, *The Guinness Book of Names, 6th edition* (Guinness Publishing, 1993)

Fry, Jonson, *The Personal Finance Pocket Book 1992-3* (NTC Publications, 1992)

Hadfield, Greg, *The Sunday Times State Schools Book* (Bloomsbury, 1993)

Hannah, Leslie, *Education, Opportunity and Business Leadership* (Foundation for Manufacturing and Industry, 1993)

Hobbes, Thomas, *Leviathan* (1651)

Independent Schools Information Service and Mori, *How and Why Parents Choose an Independent School* (ISIS/Mori, 1989, 1994)

Inland Revenue Statistics (HMSO, 1993)

Jacobs, Eric and Worcester, Robert, *We British: Britain Under the Moriscope* (Weidenfeld and Nicolson, 1990)

Jowell, Roger, Brook, Lindsay and Dowds, Lizanne (eds), *International Social Attitudes: the 10th British Social Attitudes Report* (Dartmouth, 1993)

Lex Report on Motoring (Lex Service, 1993)

Market Research Society, *Occupation Groupings: A Job Dictionary* (Market Research Society, 1991)

Marx, Karl and Engels, Friedrich, *The Communist Manifesto 1848* (Penguin, 1967)

Mitfold, Nancy (ed), *Noblesse Oblige* (Hamish Hamilton, 1956)

National Consumer Council, *Credit and Debt: The Consumer Interest* (HMSO, 1990)

Nielsen, *The Retail Pocket Book* (NTC Publications, 1993)

NOP Consumer Market Research, *Share Ownership* (NOP, 1993)

Northcott, Jim, *Britain in 2010: The Policy Studies Institute Report* (Policy Studies Institute, 1991)

O'Brien, Sarah and Ford, Rosemary, *Can We At Least Say Goodbye to Social Class* (Market Research Society conference paper, 1988)

Office of Population Censuses and Surveys, *Standard Occupational Classification, Volume 3* (HMSO, 1991)

– *1992 General Household Survey* (HMSO, 1994)

Orwell, George, *The Road to Wigan Pier* (Gollancz, 1937)

– *Down and Out in Paris and London* (Gollancz, 1937)

– *The Collected Essays, Journalism and Letters 1920-50* (Secker and Warburg, 1968)

Paxman, Jeremy, *Friends in High Places* (Michael Joseph, 1990)

Sampson, Anthony, *The Essential Anatomy of Britain* (Hodder and Stoughton, 1992)

Scase, Richard, *Class* (Open University Press, 1992)

Seebohm Rowntree, B., *Poverty and Progress* (Longman, 1941)

Shareholder Segmentation, (Proshare, 1992)

Watkins, Leslie and Worcester, Robert, *Private Opinions, Public Polls* (Thames and Hudson, 1986)

West, Richard, *An English Journey* (Chatto and Windus, 1981)

Whitehall Companion 1992-3 and 1993-4 (Dod's Publishing and Research, 1994)

Who's Who (A & C Black, 1994)

Woodford, Sue and de Zoysa, Anne, *The Good Nursery Guide* (Vermilion, 1993)

INDEX